# DEADLY AWESOME

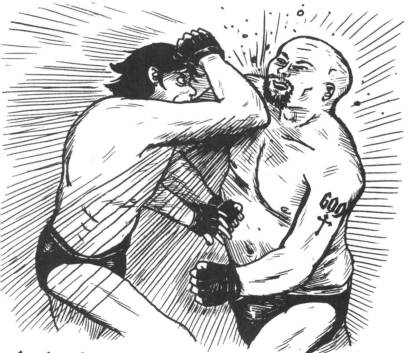

A COMPETITIVE MIXED MARTIAL ARTS MATCH
FROM THE S.C.F.C.L.
(SUPERIOR CAGE FIGHTING CHAMPIONSHIP LEAGUE)

## OFFICIAL S.C.F.C.L. RULES

- EACH MATCH LASTS FOR UP TO 3 ROUNDS, WITH EACH ROUND LASTING FIVE MINUTES AND ONE MINUTE BREAKS IN BETWEEN ROUNDS.
- THINGS THAT ARE NOT ALLOWED: HEAD BUTTING, BITING, SPITTING, POKING EYES OUT, KICKING IN THE BALLS, SMALL JOINT MANIPULATION, HOLDING THE CAGE, UNGENTLEMANLY LANGUAGE, TITTY TWISTERS, AND HAIR PULLING. FOR A COMPLETE LIST OF ACTIONS FORBIDDEN IN S.C.F.C.L. COMPETITION, PLEASE SEE THE OFFICIAL WEBSITE.
- THERE ARE FIVE WAYS TO WIN:
  1. SUBMITTING YOUR OPPONENT (WITH A SUBMISSION)
  2. KNOCKING YOUR OPPONENT OUT.
  3. YOUR OPPONENT'S CORNER "THROWS IN THE TOWEL."
  4. THE REFEREE STOPS THE FIGHT (TKO).
  5. THE JUDGES DECIDE THAT YOU ARE THE WINNER.

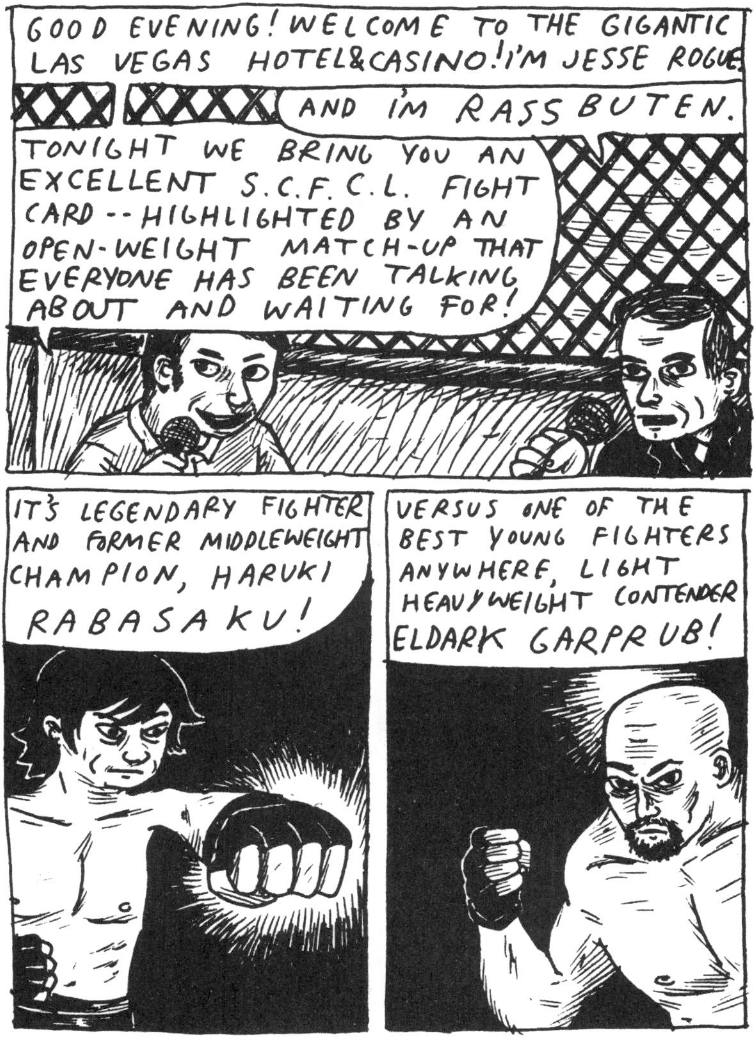
GOOD EVENING! WELCOME TO THE GIGANTIC LAS VEGAS HOTEL&CASINO! I'M JESSE ROGUE.
AND I'M RASSBUTEN.
TONIGHT WE BRING YOU AN EXCELLENT S.C.F.C.L. FIGHT CARD -- HIGHLIGHTED BY AN OPEN-WEIGHT MATCH-UP THAT EVERYONE HAS BEEN TALKING ABOUT AND WAITING FOR!
IT'S LEGENDARY FIGHTER AND FORMER MIDDLEWEIGHT CHAMPION, HARUKI RABASAKU!
VERSUS ONE OF THE BEST YOUNG FIGHTERS ANYWHERE, LIGHT HEAVYWEIGHT CONTENDER ELDARK GARPRUB!

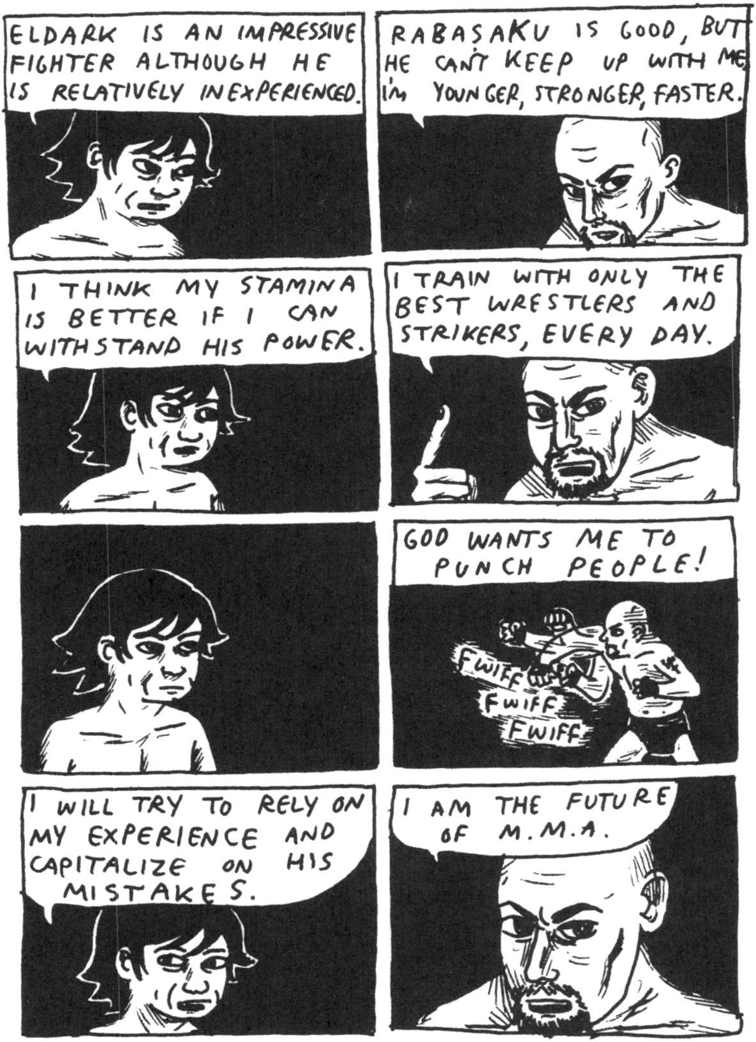
ELDARK IS AN IMPRESSIVE FIGHTER ALTHOUGH HE IS RELATIVELY INEXPERIENCED.
RABASAKU IS GOOD, BUT HE CAN'T KEEP UP WITH ME. I'M YOUNGER, STRONGER, FASTER.
I THINK MY STAMINA IS BETTER IF I CAN WITHSTAND HIS POWER.
I TRAIN WITH ONLY THE BEST WRESTLERS AND STRIKERS, EVERY DAY.
GOD WANTS ME TO PUNCH PEOPLE!
FWIFF
FWIFF
FWIFF
I WILL TRY TO RELY ON MY EXPERIENCE AND CAPITALIZE ON HIS MISTAKES.
I AM THE FUTURE OF M.M.A.

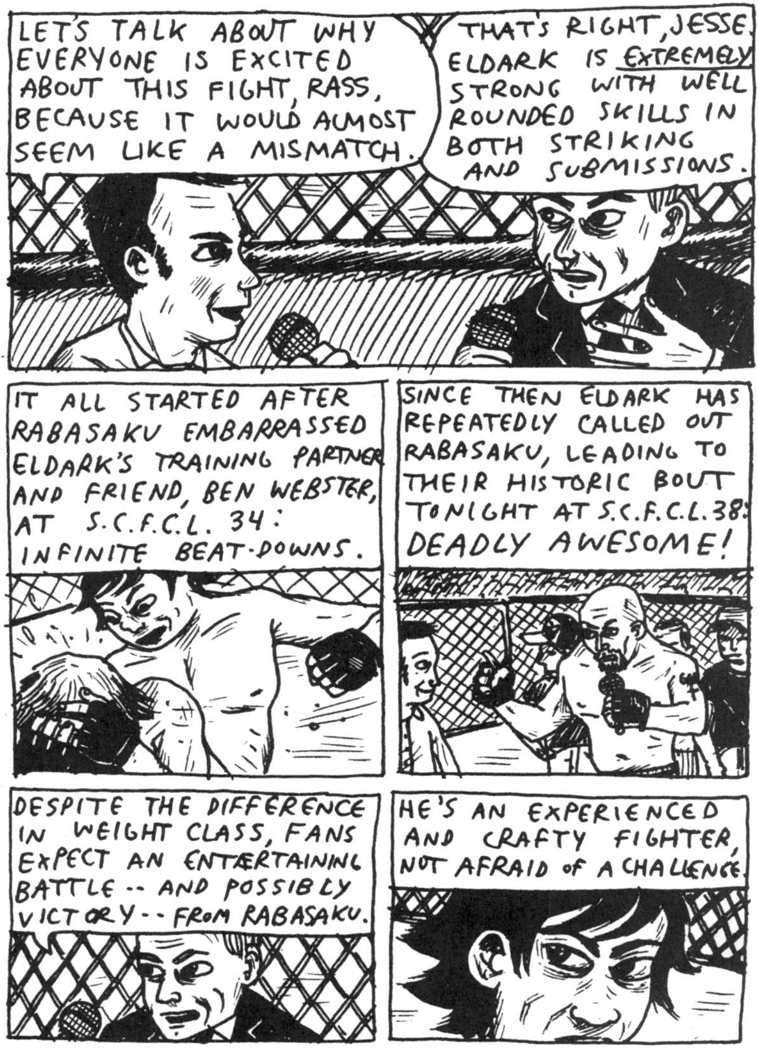
LET'S TALK ABOUT WHY EVERYONE IS EXCITED ABOUT THIS FIGHT, RASS, BECAUSE IT WOULD ALMOST SEEM LIKE A MISMATCH.
THAT'S RIGHT, JESSE. ELDARK IS EXTREMELY STRONG WITH WELL ROUNDED SKILLS IN BOTH STRIKING AND SUBMISSIONS.
IT ALL STARTED AFTER RABASAKU EMBARRASSED ELDARK'S TRAINING PARTNER AND FRIEND, BEN WEBSTER, AT S.C.F.C.L. 34: INFINITE BEAT-DOWNS.
SINCE THEN ELDARK HAS REPEATEDLY CALLED OUT RABASAKU, LEADING TO THEIR HISTORIC BOUT TONIGHT AT S.C.F.C.L. 38: DEADLY AWESOME!
DESPITE THE DIFFERENCE IN WEIGHT CLASS, FANS EXPECT AN ENTERTAINING BATTLE -- AND POSSIBLY VICTORY -- FROM RABASAKU.
HE'S AN EXPERIENCED AND CRAFTY FIGHTER, NOT AFRAID OF A CHALLENGE.

DESPITE HIS AGE, AND TWO LOSSES IN HIS LAST FIVE FIGHTS, RABASAKU IS STILL CONSIDERED ONE OF THE BEST MIDDLEWEIGHT FIGHTERS, AN ALWAYS DANGEROUS OPPONENT.

OOOF!

IN HIS LAST FIGHT, RABASAKU WEATHERED TWO ROUNDS OF PUNISHING DOMINATION BY RISING STAR MARTIN NAKAMURA...

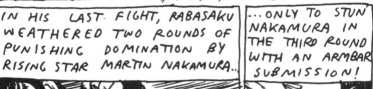

...ONLY TO STUN NAKAMURA IN THE THIRD ROUND WITH AN ARMBAR SUBMISSION!

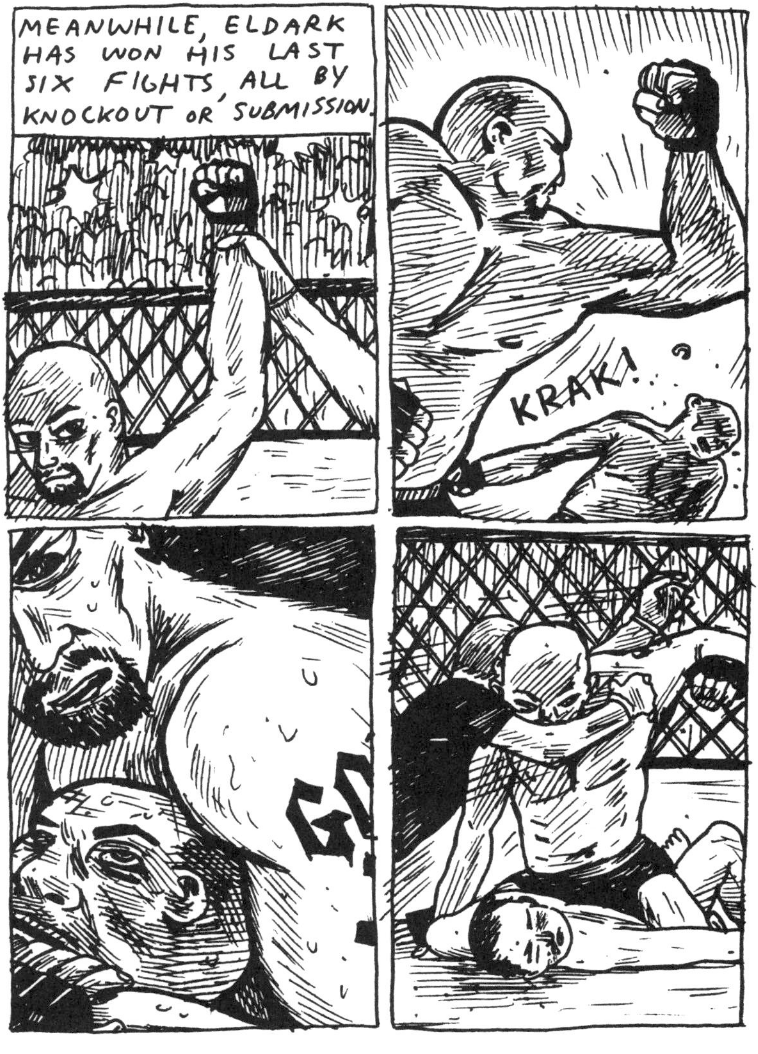
MEANWHILE, ELDARK HAS WON HIS LAST SIX FIGHTS, ALL BY KNOCKOUT OR SUBMISSION.
KRAK!

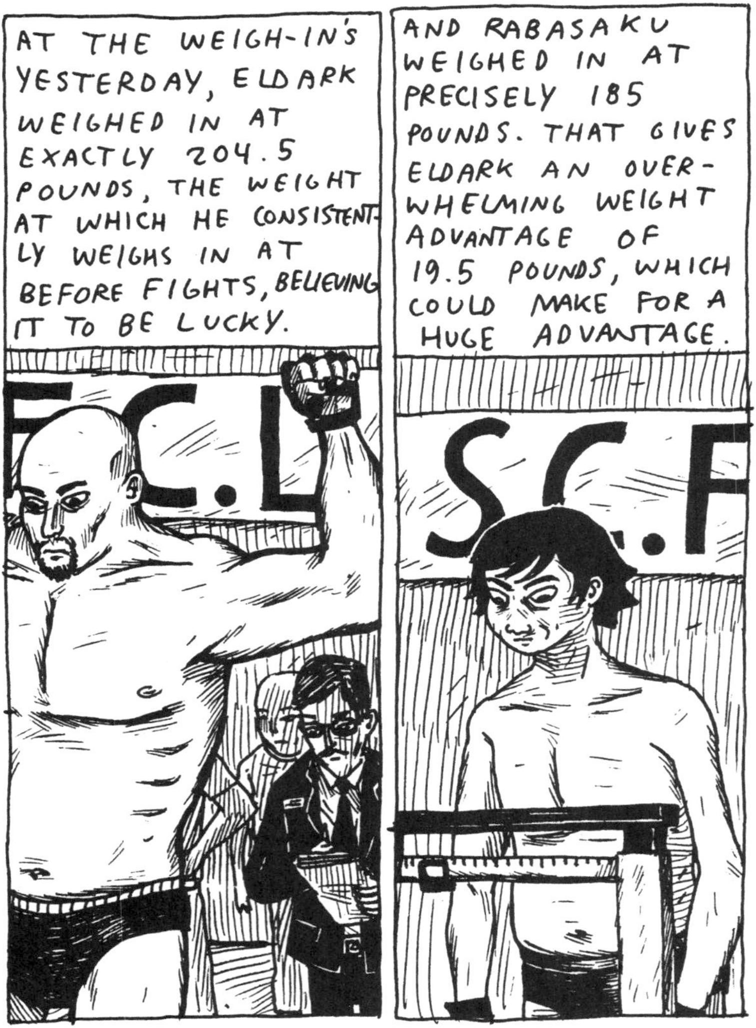
AT THE WEIGH-IN'S YESTERDAY, ELDARK WEIGHED IN AT EXACTLY 204.5 POUNDS, THE WEIGHT AT WHICH HE CONSISTENTLY WEIGHS IN AT BEFORE FIGHTS, BELIEVING IT TO BE LUCKY.
AND RABASAKU WEIGHED IN AT PRECISELY 185 POUNDS. THAT GIVES ELDARK AN OVERWHELMING WEIGHT ADVANTAGE OF 19.5 POUNDS, WHICH COULD MAKE FOR A HUGE ADVANTAGE.

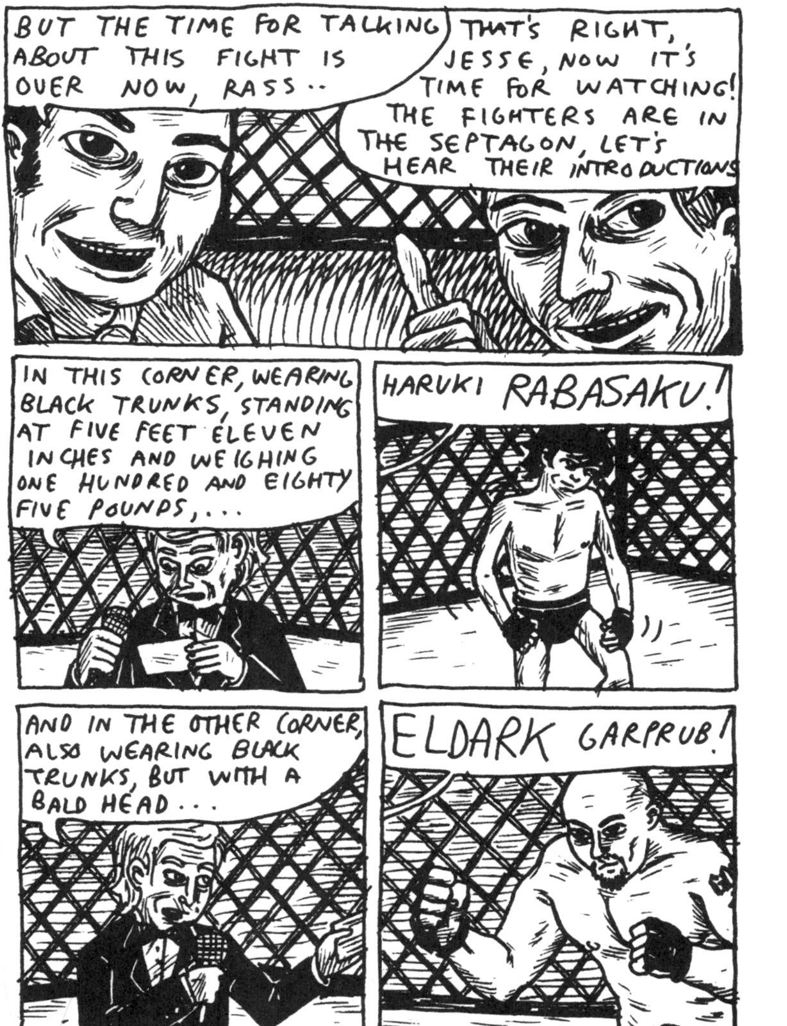
BUT THE TIME FOR TALKING ABOUT THIS FIGHT IS OVER NOW, RASS..
THAT'S RIGHT, JESSE, NOW IT'S TIME FOR WATCHING! THE FIGHTERS ARE IN THE SEPTAGON, LET'S HEAR THEIR INTRODUCTIONS
IN THIS CORNER, WEARING BLACK TRUNKS, STANDING AT FIVE FEET ELEVEN INCHES AND WEIGHING ONE HUNDRED AND EIGHTY FIVE POUNDS,...
HARUKI RABASAKU!
AND IN THE OTHER CORNER, ALSO WEARING BLACK TRUNKS, BUT WITH A BALD HEAD...
ELDARK GARPRUB!

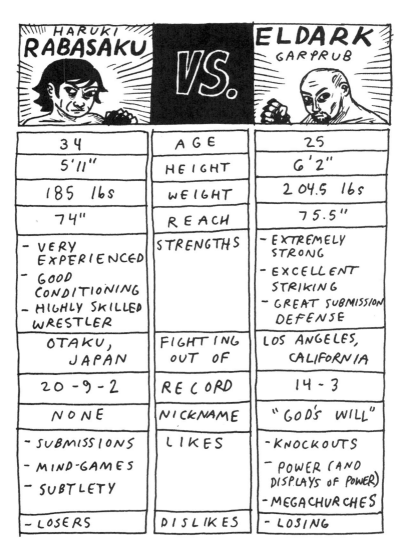

# HARUKI RABASAKU

## VS.

# ELDARK GARPRUB

| HARUKI RABASAKU | | ELDARK GARPRUB |
|---|---|---|
| 34 | AGE | 25 |
| 5'11" | HEIGHT | 6'2" |
| 185 lbs | WEIGHT | 204.5 lbs |
| 74" | REACH | 75.5" |
| - VERY EXPERIENCED<br>- GOOD CONDITIONING<br>- HIGHLY SKILLED WRESTLER | STRENGTHS | - EXTREMELY STRONG<br>- EXCELLENT STRIKING<br>- GREAT SUBMISSION DEFENSE |
| OTAKU, JAPAN | FIGHTING OUT OF | LOS ANGELES, CALIFORNIA |
| 20-9-2 | RECORD | 14-3 |
| NONE | NICKNAME | "GOD'S WILL" |
| - SUBMISSIONS<br>- MIND-GAMES<br>- SUBTLETY | LIKES | - KNOCKOUTS<br>- POWER (AND DISPLAYS OF POWER)<br>- MEGACHURCHES |
| - LOSERS | DISLIKES | - LOSING |

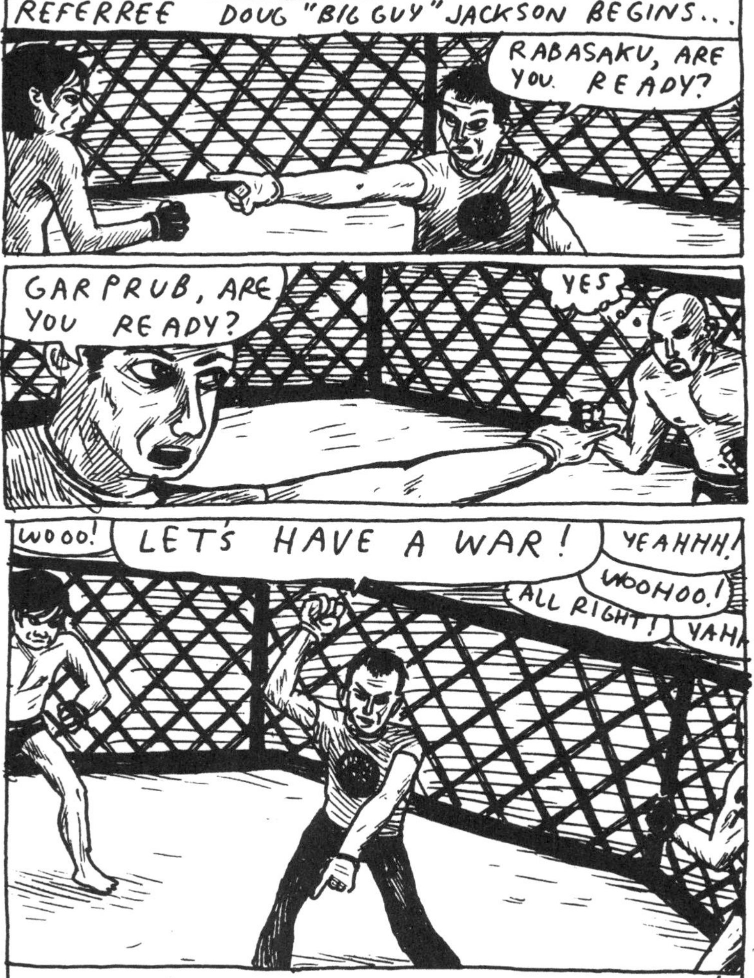
REFERREE DOUG "BIG GUY" JACKSON BEGINS...
RABASAKU, ARE YOU READY?
GARPRUB, ARE YOU READY?
YES
WOOO!
LET'S HAVE A WAR!
YEAHHH!
WOOHOO!
ALL RIGHT!
YAH
THE CROWD CHEERS WILDLY WITH EXCITEMENT!

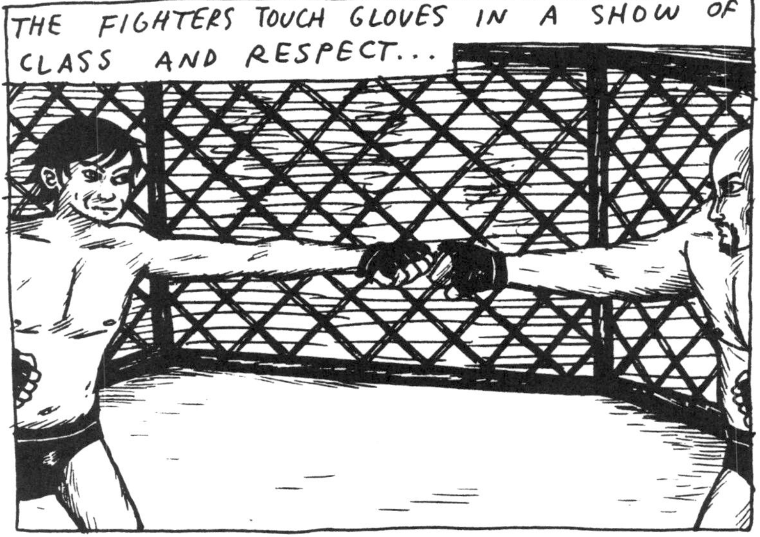
THE FIGHTERS TOUCH GLOVES IN A SHOW OF CLASS AND RESPECT...

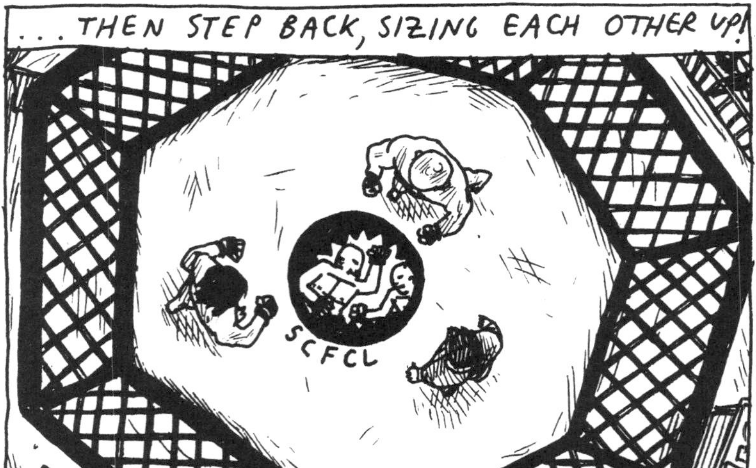
...THEN STEP BACK, SIZING EACH OTHER UP!
SCFCL

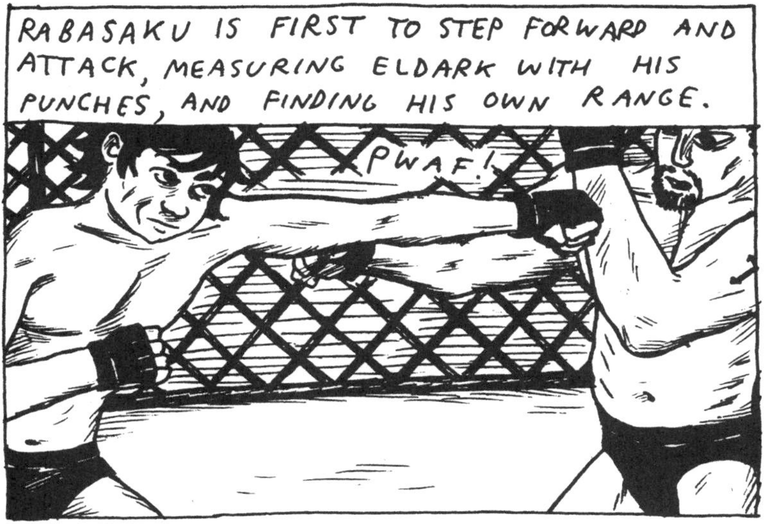
RABASAKU IS FIRST TO STEP FORWARD AND ATTACK, MEASURING ELDARK WITH HIS PUNCHES, AND FINDING HIS OWN RANGE.
PWAF!

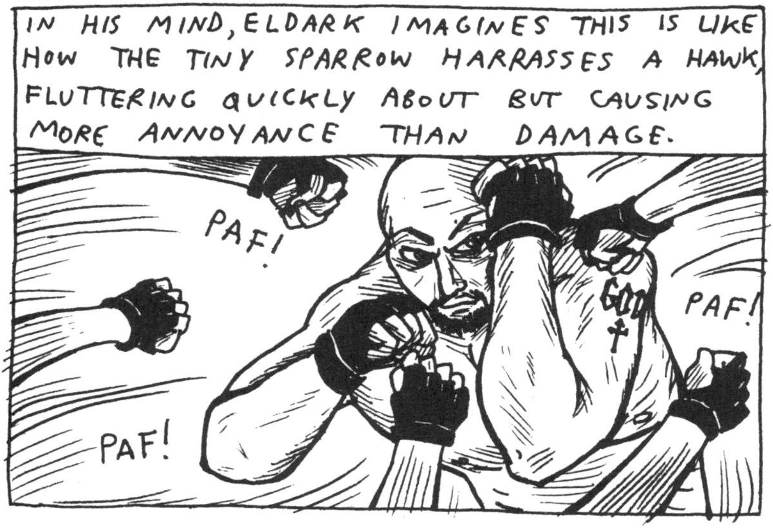
IN HIS MIND, ELDARK IMAGINES THIS IS LIKE HOW THE TINY SPARROW HARRASSES A HAWK, FLUTTERING QUICKLY ABOUT BUT CAUSING MORE ANNOYANCE THAN DAMAGE.
PAF!
PAF!
PAF!

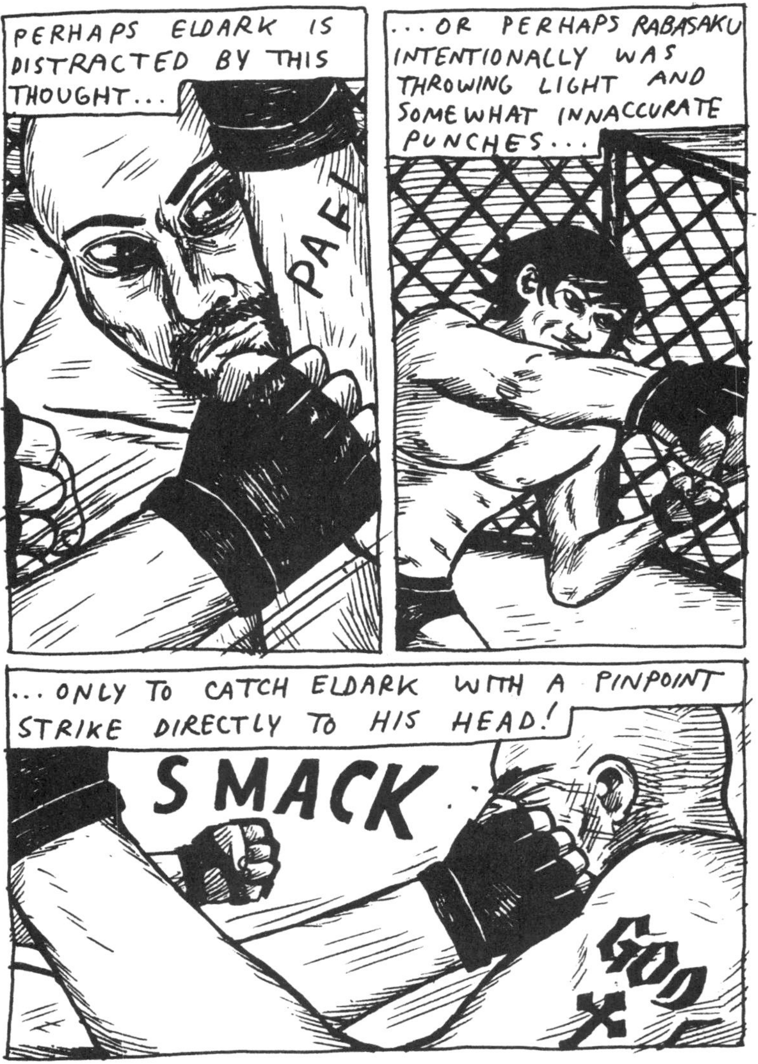
PERHAPS ELDARK IS DISTRACTED BY THIS THOUGHT...
PAF!
...OR PERHAPS RABASAKU INTENTIONALLY WAS THROWING LIGHT AND SOMEWHAT INNACCURATE PUNCHES...
...ONLY TO CATCH ELDARK WITH A PINPOINT STRIKE DIRECTLY TO HIS HEAD!
SMACK
GOD

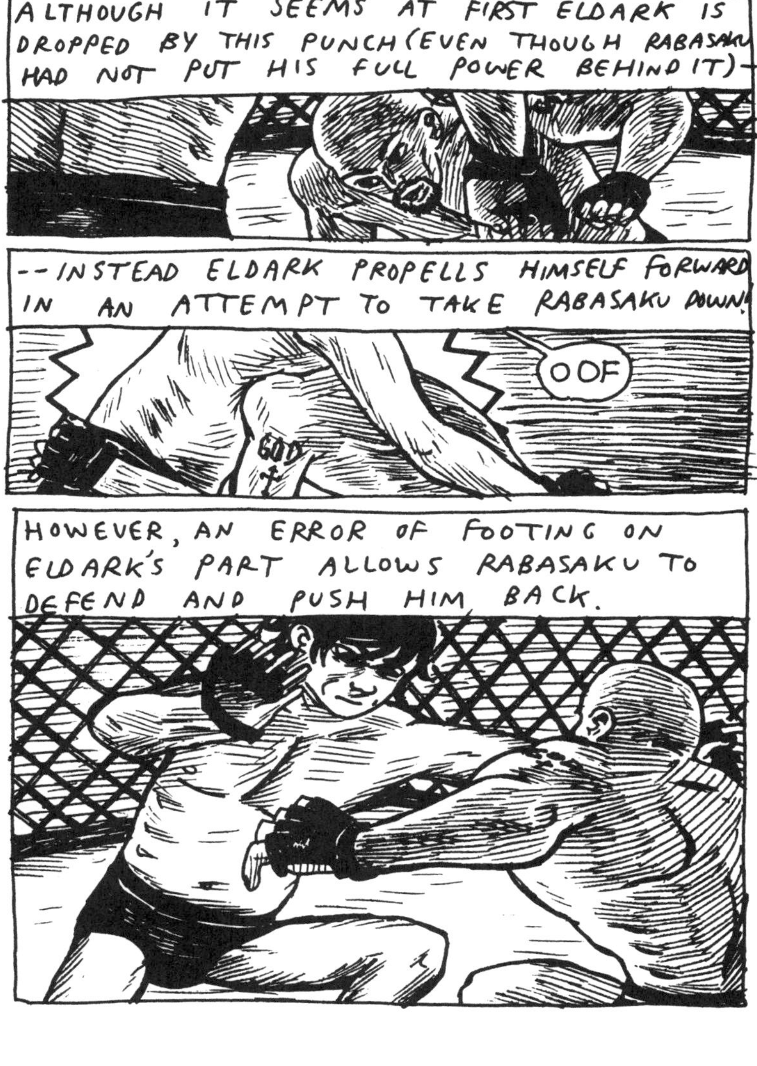
ALTHOUGH IT SEEMS AT FIRST ELDARK IS DROPPED BY THIS PUNCH (EVEN THOUGH RABASAKU HAD NOT PUT HIS FULL POWER BEHIND IT)-
--INSTEAD ELDARK PROPELLS HIMSELF FORWARD IN AN ATTEMPT TO TAKE RABASAKU DOWN!
OOF
GOD
HOWEVER, AN ERROR OF FOOTING ON ELDARK'S PART ALLOWS RABASAKU TO DEFEND AND PUSH HIM BACK.

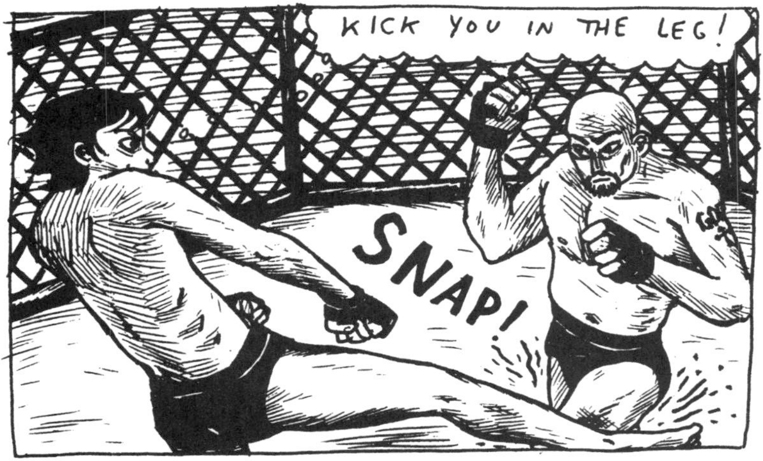
KICK YOU IN THE LEG!
SNAP!

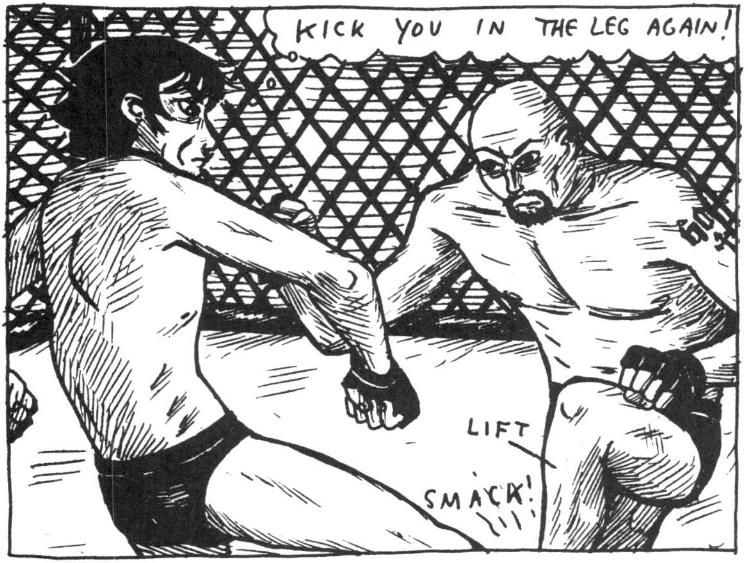
KICK YOU IN THE LEG AGAIN!
LIFT
SMACK!

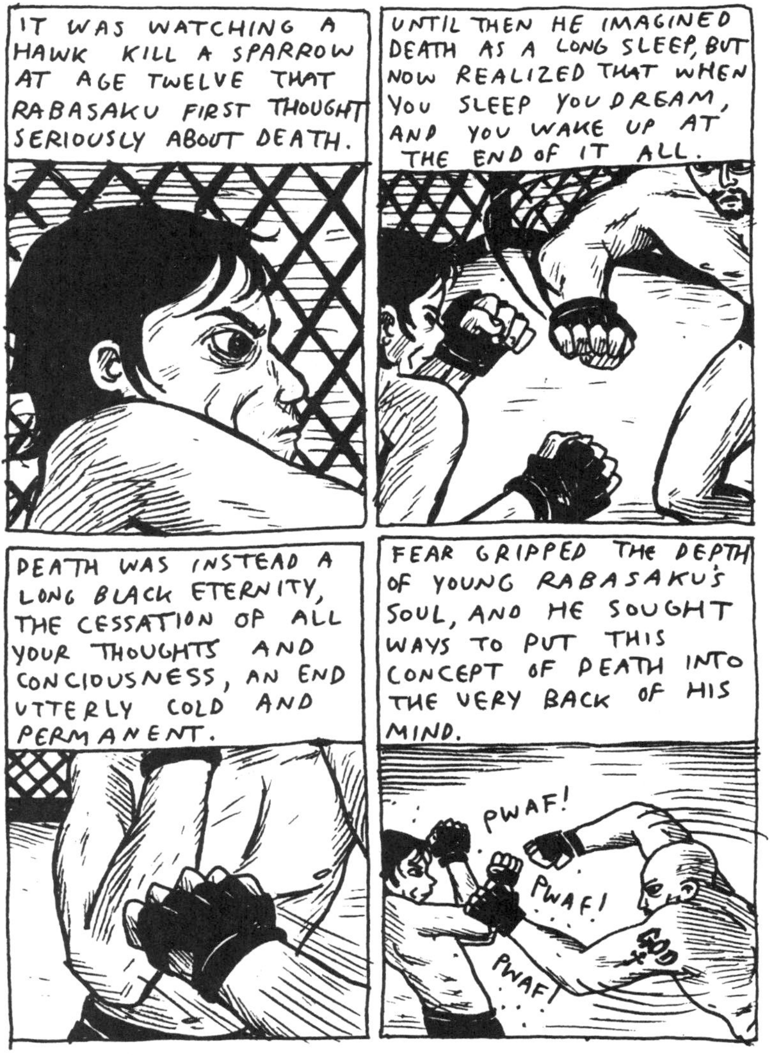
IT WAS WATCHING A HAWK KILL A SPARROW AT AGE TWELVE THAT RABASAKU FIRST THOUGHT SERIOUSLY ABOUT DEATH.
UNTIL THEN HE IMAGINED DEATH AS A LONG SLEEP, BUT NOW REALIZED THAT WHEN YOU SLEEP YOU DREAM, AND YOU WAKE UP AT THE END OF IT ALL.
DEATH WAS INSTEAD A LONG BLACK ETERNITY, THE CESSATION OF ALL YOUR THOUGHTS AND CONCIOUSNESS, AN END UTTERLY COLD AND PERMANENT.
FEAR GRIPPED THE DEPTH OF YOUNG RABASAKU'S SOUL, AND HE SOUGHT WAYS TO PUT THIS CONCEPT OF DEATH INTO THE VERY BACK OF HIS MIND.
PWAF!
PWAF!
PWAF!
GOD

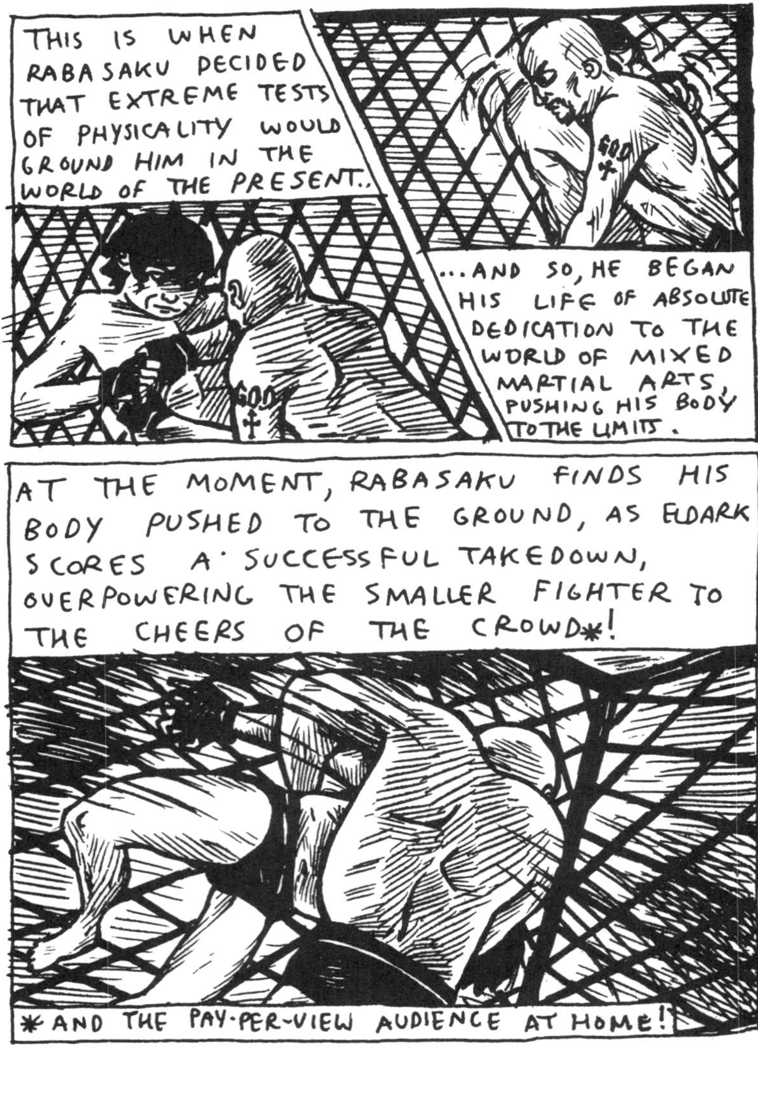
THIS IS WHEN RABASAKU DECIDED THAT EXTREME TESTS OF PHYSICALITY WOULD GROUND HIM IN THE WORLD OF THE PRESENT...
...AND SO, HE BEGAN HIS LIFE OF ABSOLUTE DEDICATION TO THE WORLD OF MIXED MARTIAL ARTS, PUSHING HIS BODY TO THE LIMITS.
AT THE MOMENT, RABASAKU FINDS HIS BODY PUSHED TO THE GROUND, AS ELDARK SCORES A SUCCESSFUL TAKEDOWN, OVERPOWERING THE SMALLER FIGHTER TO THE CHEERS OF THE CROWD*!
*AND THE PAY-PER-VIEW AUDIENCE AT HOME!

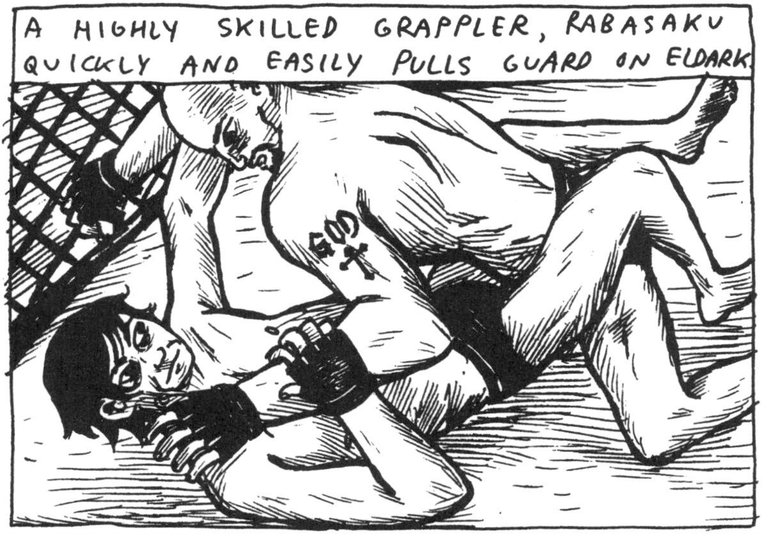
A HIGHLY SKILLED GRAPPLER, RABASAKU QUICKLY AND EASILY PULLS GUARD ON ELDARK.

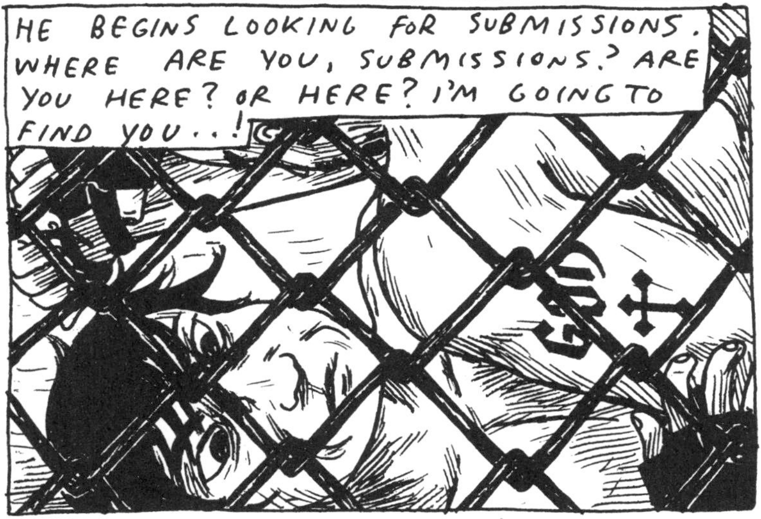
HE BEGINS LOOKING FOR SUBMISSIONS. WHERE ARE YOU, SUBMISSIONS? ARE YOU HERE? OR HERE? I'M GOING TO FIND YOU...!

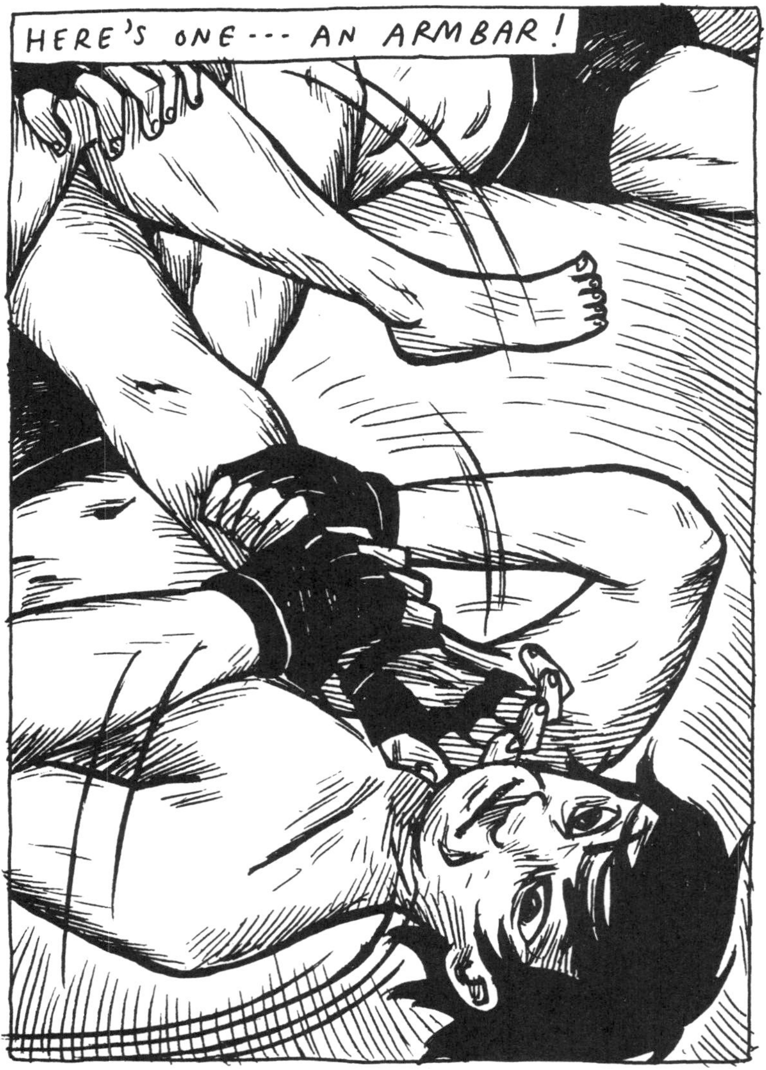
HERE'S ONE --- AN ARMBAR!

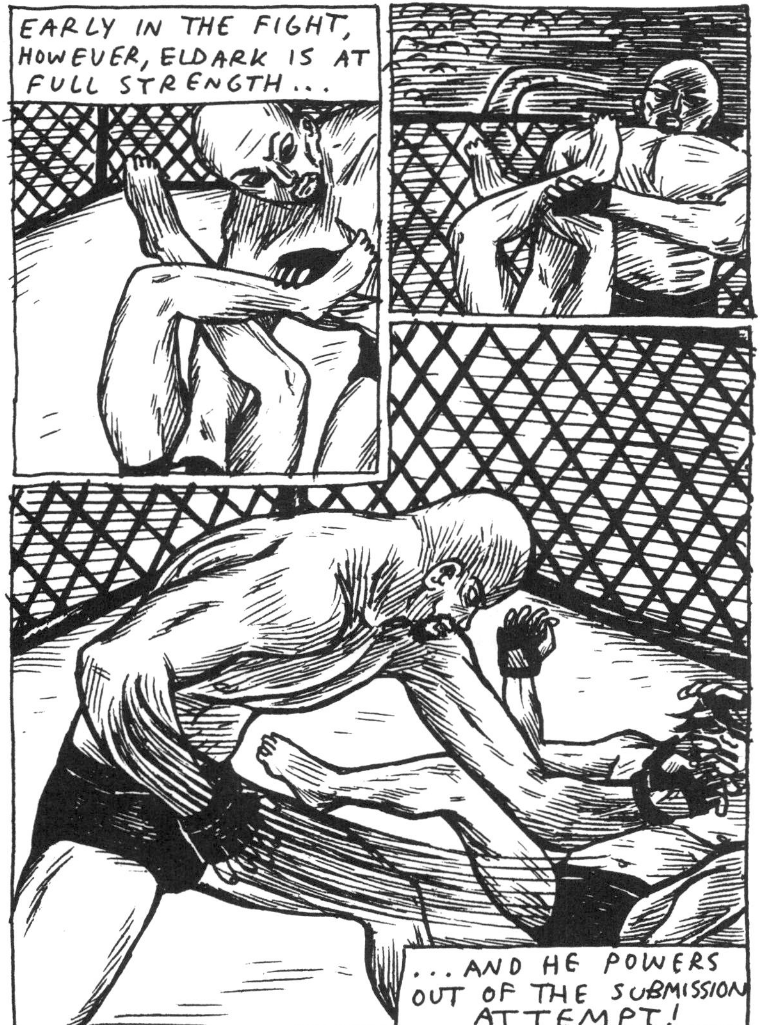
EARLY IN THE FIGHT, HOWEVER, ELDARK IS AT FULL STRENGTH...
...AND HE POWERS OUT OF THE SUBMISSION ATTEMPT!

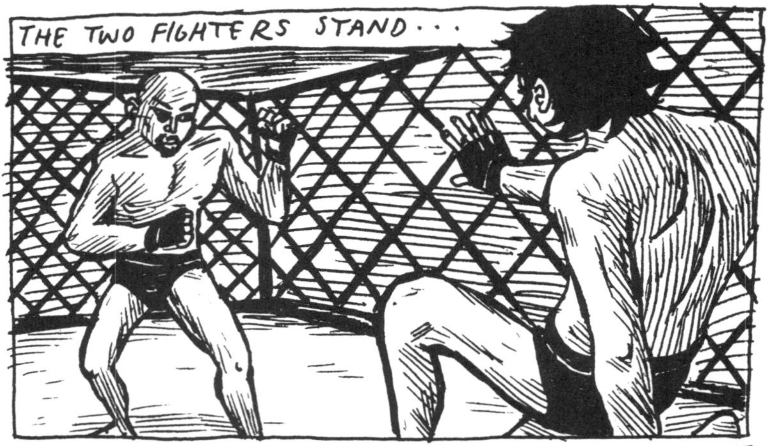
THE TWO FIGHTERS STAND...

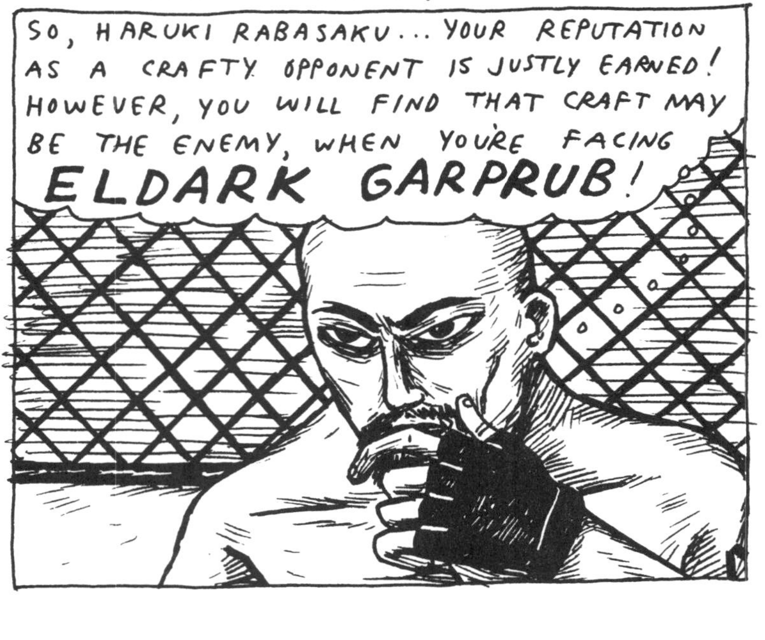
SO, HARUKI RABASAKU... YOUR REPUTATION AS A CRAFTY OPPONENT IS JUSTLY EARNED! HOWEVER, YOU WILL FIND THAT CRAFT MAY BE THE ENEMY, WHEN YOU'RE FACING
ELDARK GARPRUB!

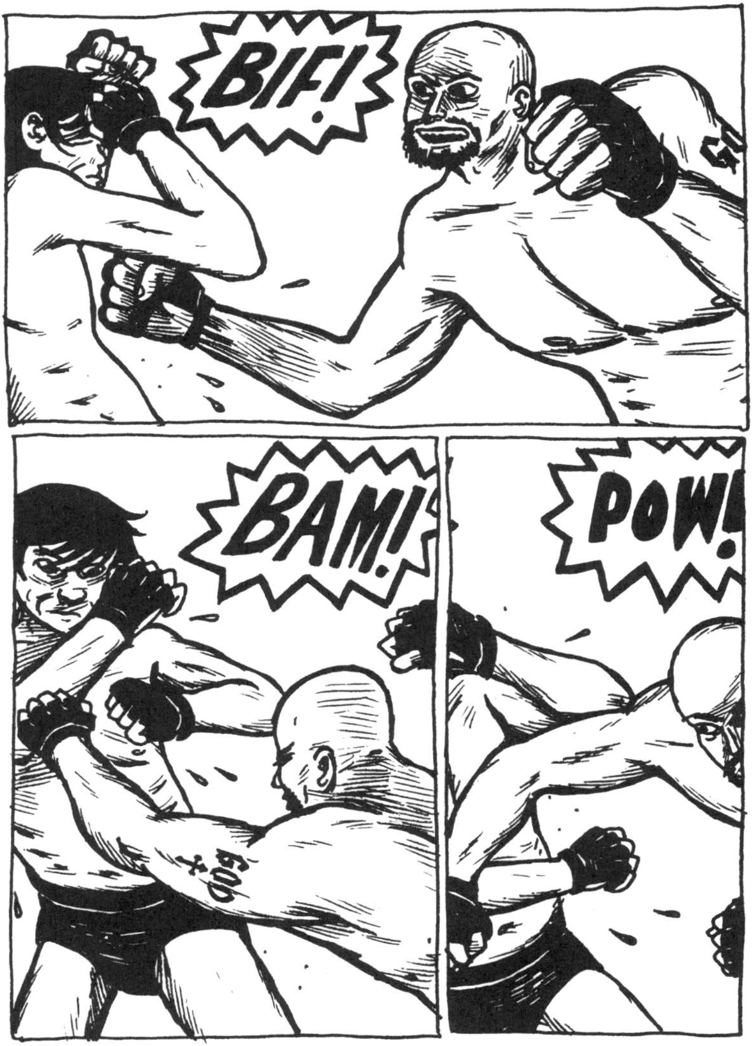
BIF!
BAM!
GOD
POW!

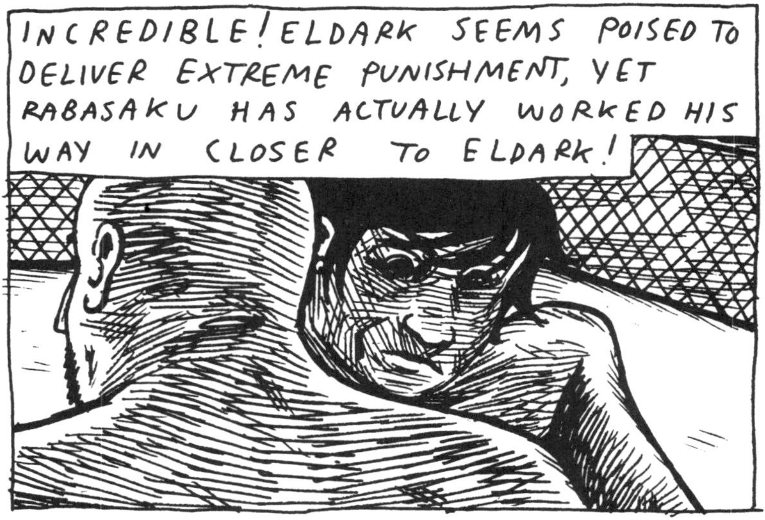
INCREDIBLE! ELDARK SEEMS POISED TO DELIVER EXTREME PUNISHMENT, YET RABASAKU HAS ACTUALLY WORKED HIS WAY IN CLOSER TO ELDARK!

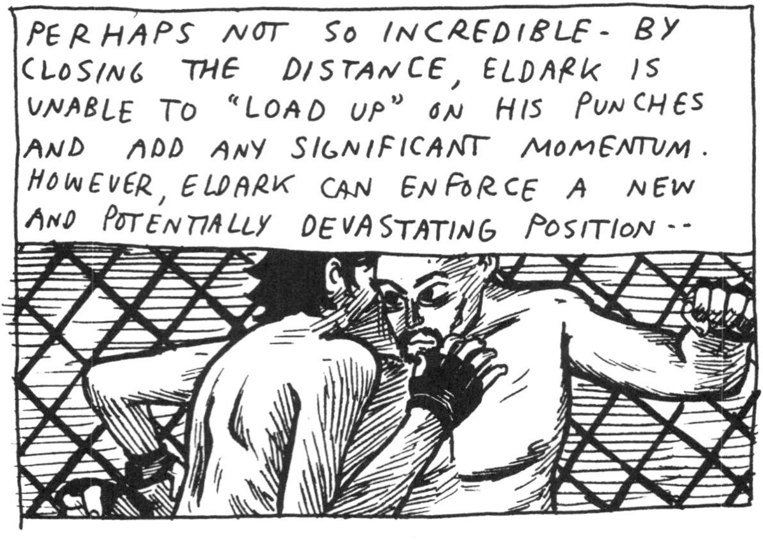
PERHAPS NOT SO INCREDIBLE - BY CLOSING THE DISTANCE, ELDARK IS UNABLE TO "LOAD UP" ON HIS PUNCHES AND ADD ANY SIGNIFICANT MOMENTUM. HOWEVER, ELDARK CAN ENFORCE A NEW AND POTENTIALLY DEVASTATING POSITION --

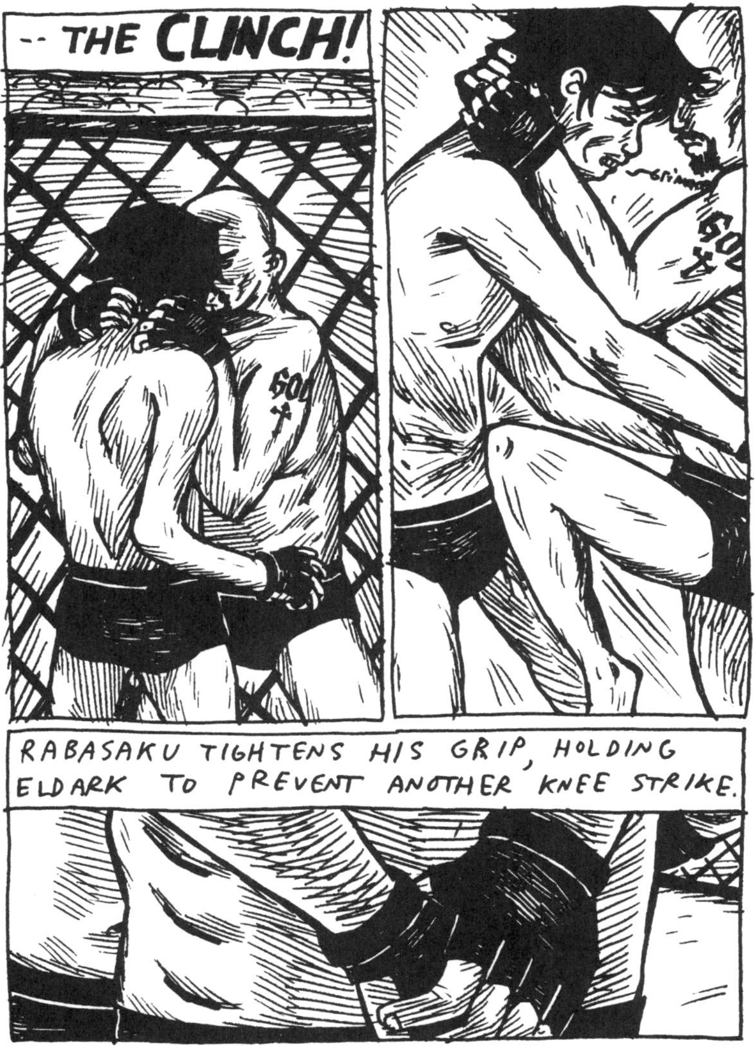
-- THE CLINCH!
RABASAKU TIGHTENS HIS GRIP, HOLDING ELDARK TO PREVENT ANOTHER KNEE STRIKE.

AS A CHILD, I MISUNDERSTOOD THE PHRASE "THE BIGGER THEY ARE, THE HARDER THEY FALL." I THOUGHT IT MEANT THAT WHEN THEY WERE BIGGER, IT WAS HARDER AND MUCH LESS LIKELY FOR THEM TO FALL. BIGGER WAS STRONGER AND HARDER TO TAKE DOWN..

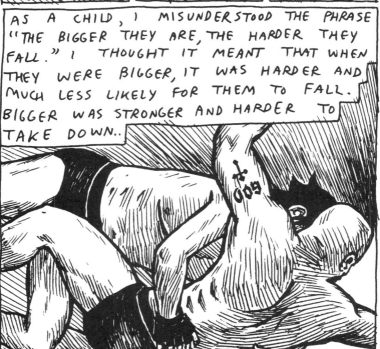

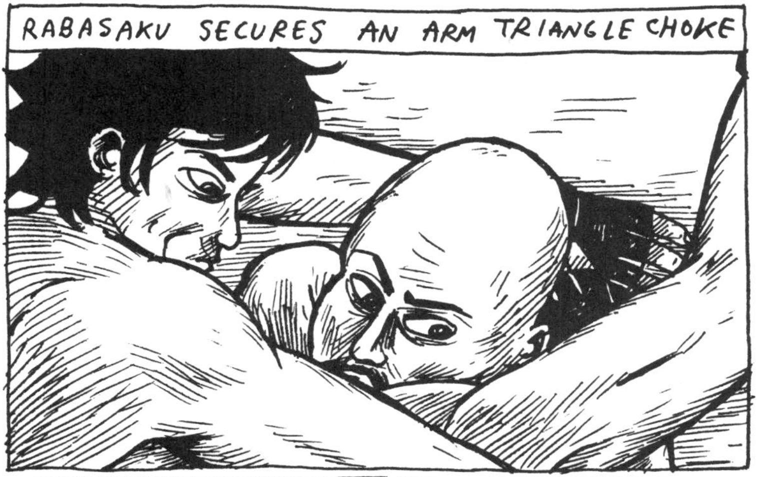
RABASAKU SECURES AN ARM TRIANGLE CHOKE

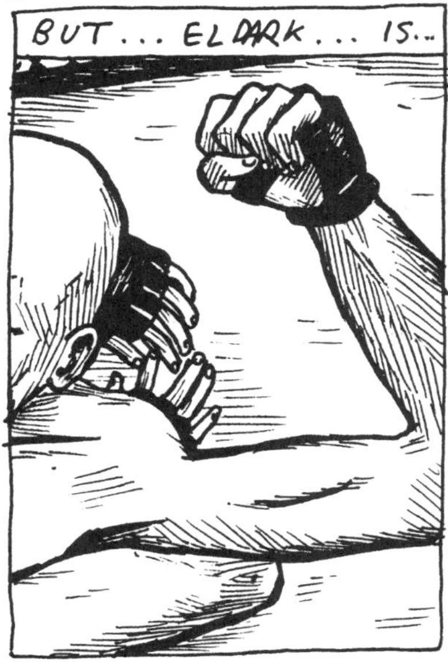
BUT... EL DARK... IS...

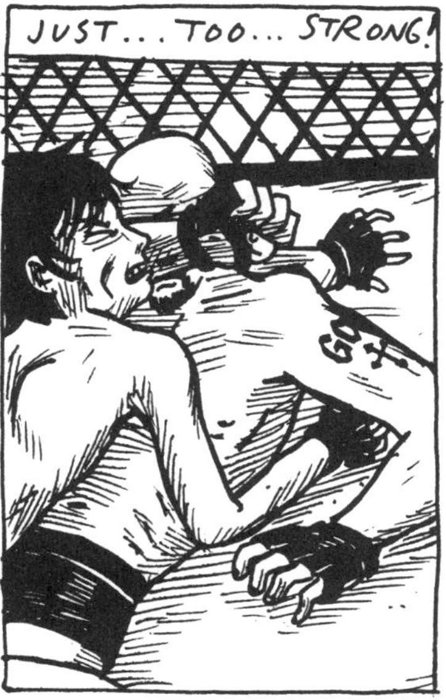
JUST... TOO... STRONG!
GO

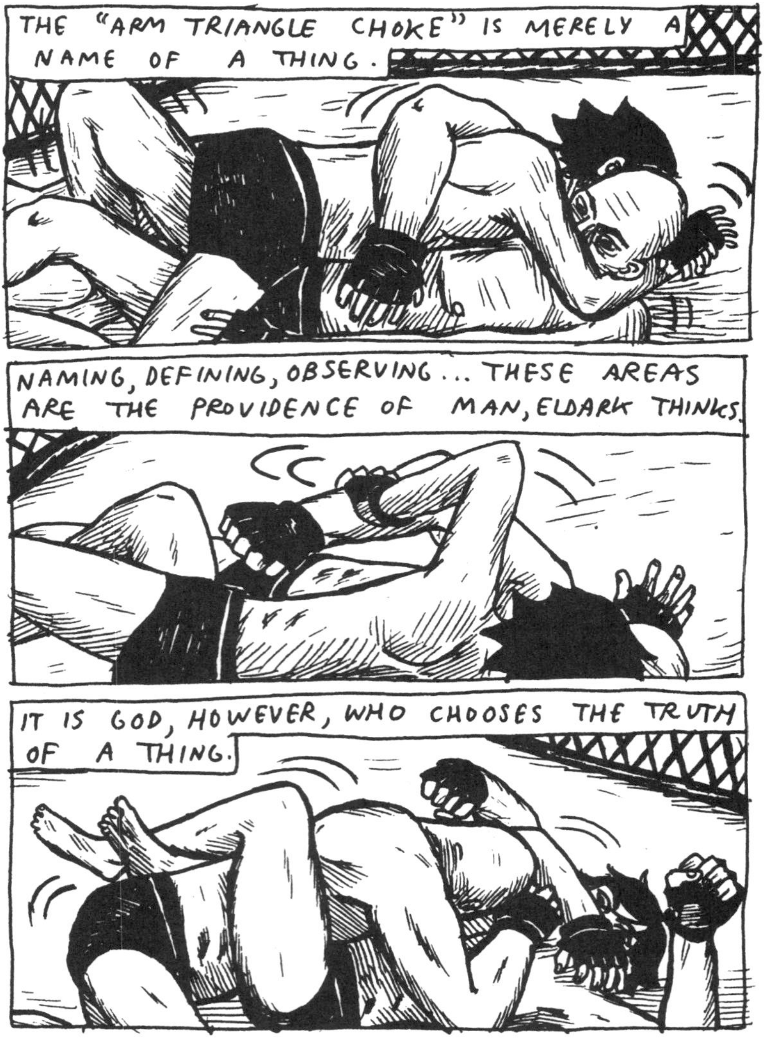
THE "ARM TRIANGLE CHOKE" IS MERELY A NAME OF A THING.
NAMING, DEFINING, OBSERVING... THESE AREAS ARE THE PROVIDENCE OF MAN, ELDARK THINKS.
IT IS GOD, HOWEVER, WHO CHOOSES THE TRUTH OF A THING.

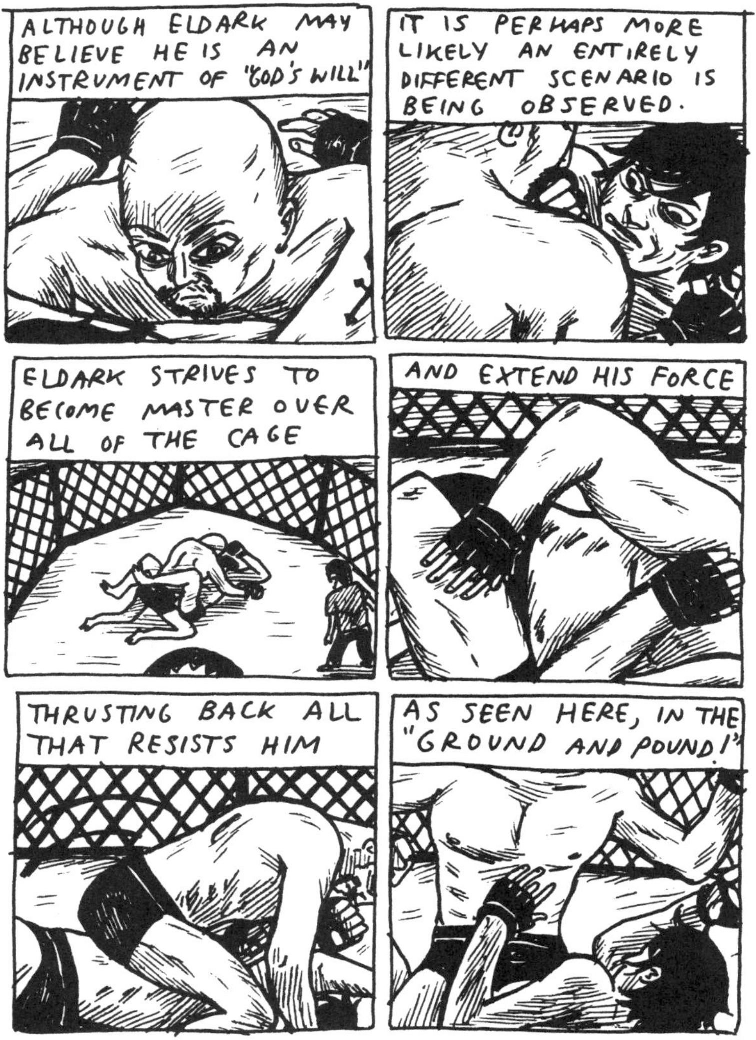

ALTHOUGH ELDARK MAY BELIEVE HE IS AN INSTRUMENT OF "GOD'S WILL"
IT IS PERHAPS MORE LIKELY AN ENTIRELY DIFFERENT SCENARIO IS BEING OBSERVED.
ELDARK STRIVES TO BECOME MASTER OVER ALL OF THE CAGE
AND EXTEND HIS FORCE
THRUSTING BACK ALL THAT RESISTS HIM
AS SEEN HERE, IN THE "GROUND AND POUND!"

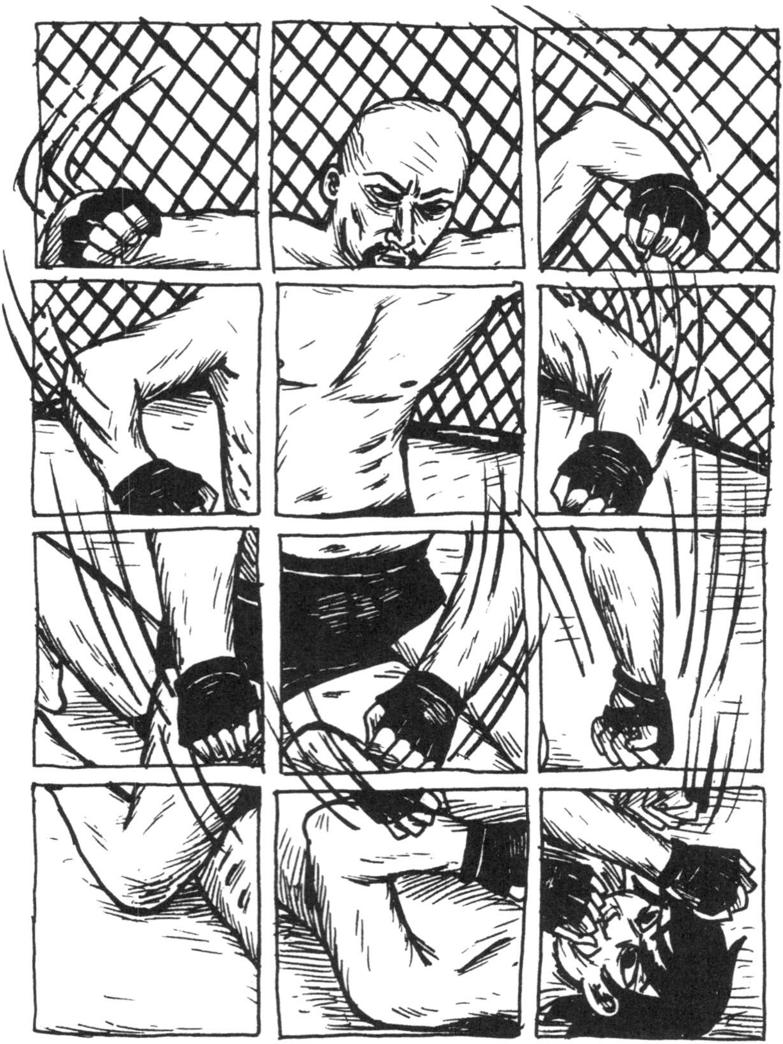

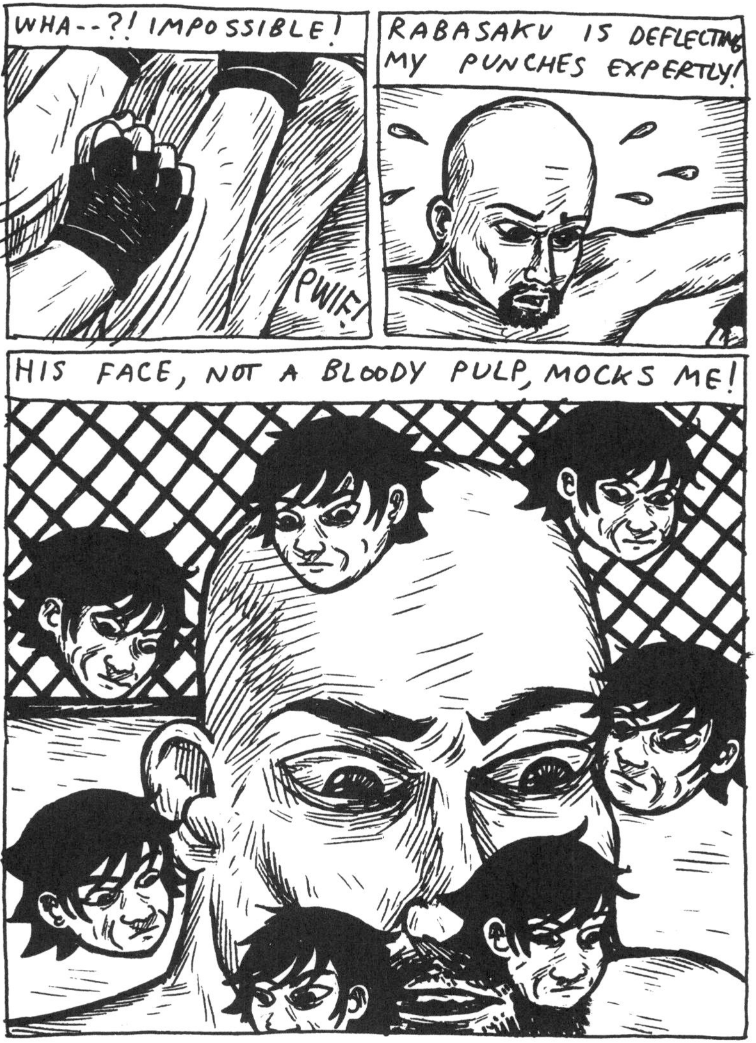
WHA--?! IMPOSSIBLE!
PWIF!
RABASAKU IS DEFLECTING MY PUNCHES EXPERTLY!
HIS FACE, NOT A BLOODY PULP, MOCKS ME!

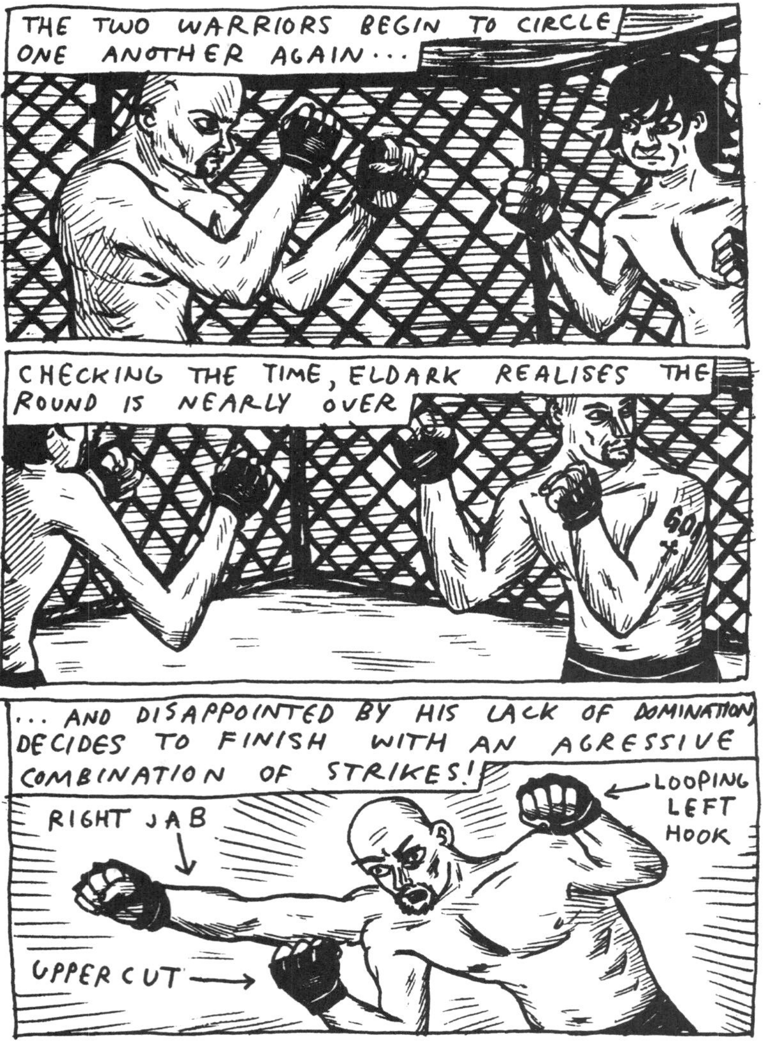
THE TWO WARRIORS BEGIN TO CIRCLE ONE ANOTHER AGAIN...
CHECKING THE TIME, ELDARK REALISES THE ROUND IS NEARLY OVER
... AND DISAPPOINTED BY HIS LACK OF DOMINATION, DECIDES TO FINISH WITH AN AGRESSIVE COMBINATION OF STRIKES!
RIGHT JAB
LOOPING LEFT HOOK
UPPERCUT

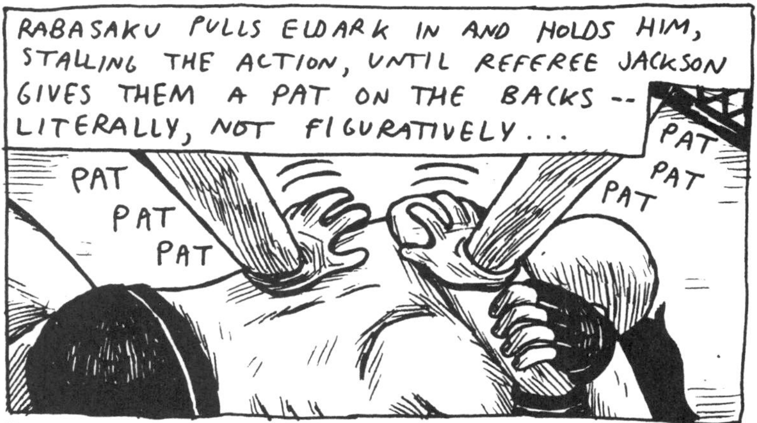
RABASAKU PULLS ELDARK IN AND HOLDS HIM, STALLING THE ACTION, UNTIL REFEREE JACKSON GIVES THEM A PAT ON THE BACKS -- LITERALLY, NOT FIGURATIVELY...
PAT PAT PAT
PAT PAT PAT

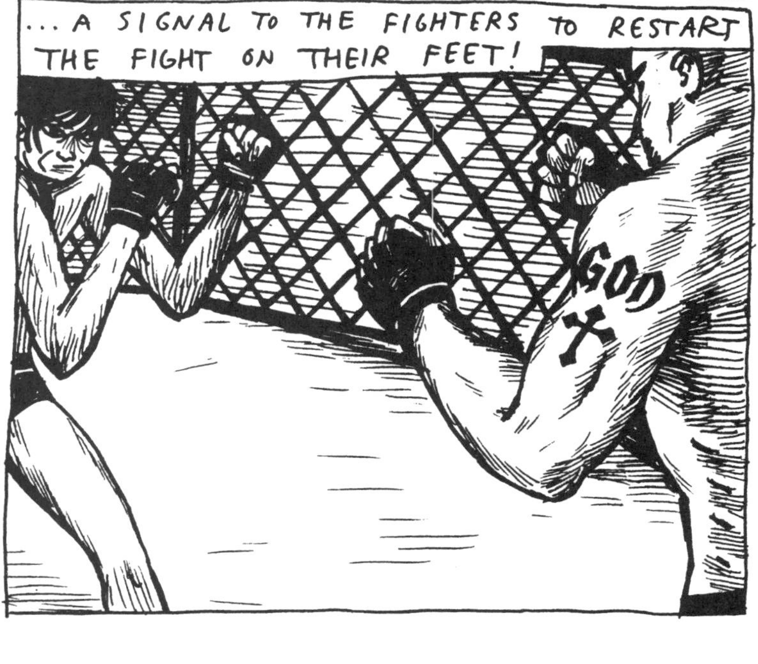
... A SIGNAL TO THE FIGHTERS TO RESTART THE FIGHT ON THEIR FEET!
GOD

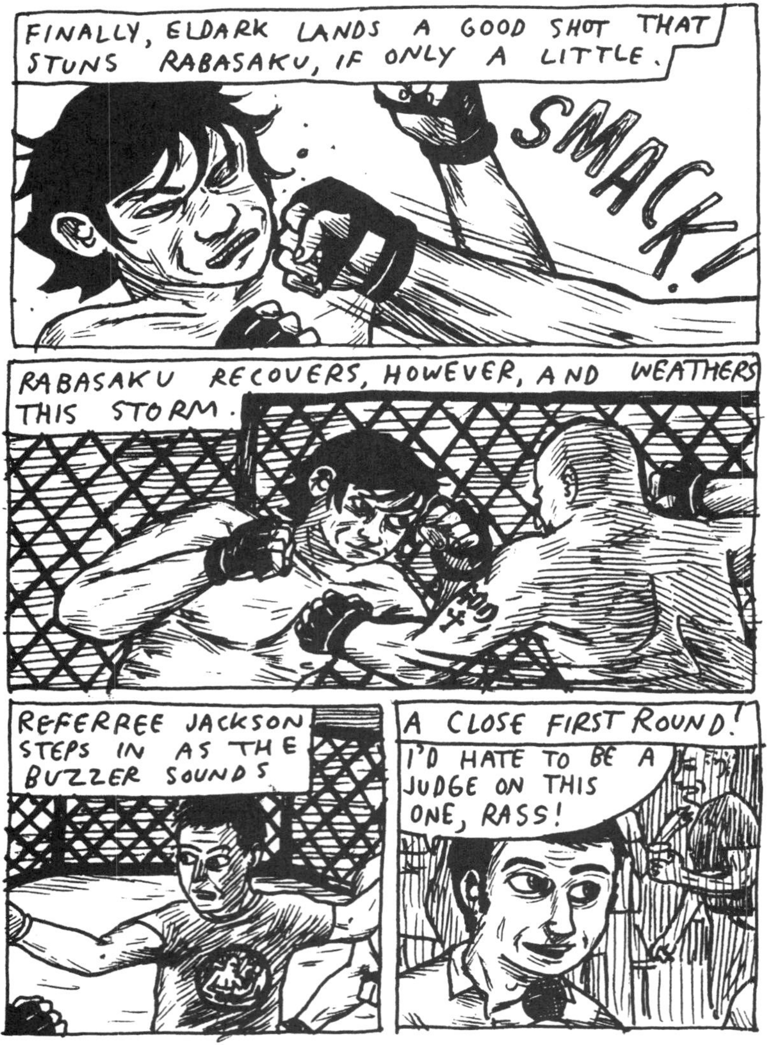
FINALLY, ELDARK LANDS A GOOD SHOT THAT STUNS RABASAKU, IF ONLY A LITTLE.
SMACK!
RABASAKU RECOVERS, HOWEVER, AND WEATHERS THIS STORM.
REFERREE JACKSON STEPS IN AS THE BUZZER SOUNDS
A CLOSE FIRST ROUND!
I'D HATE TO BE A JUDGE ON THIS ONE, RASS!

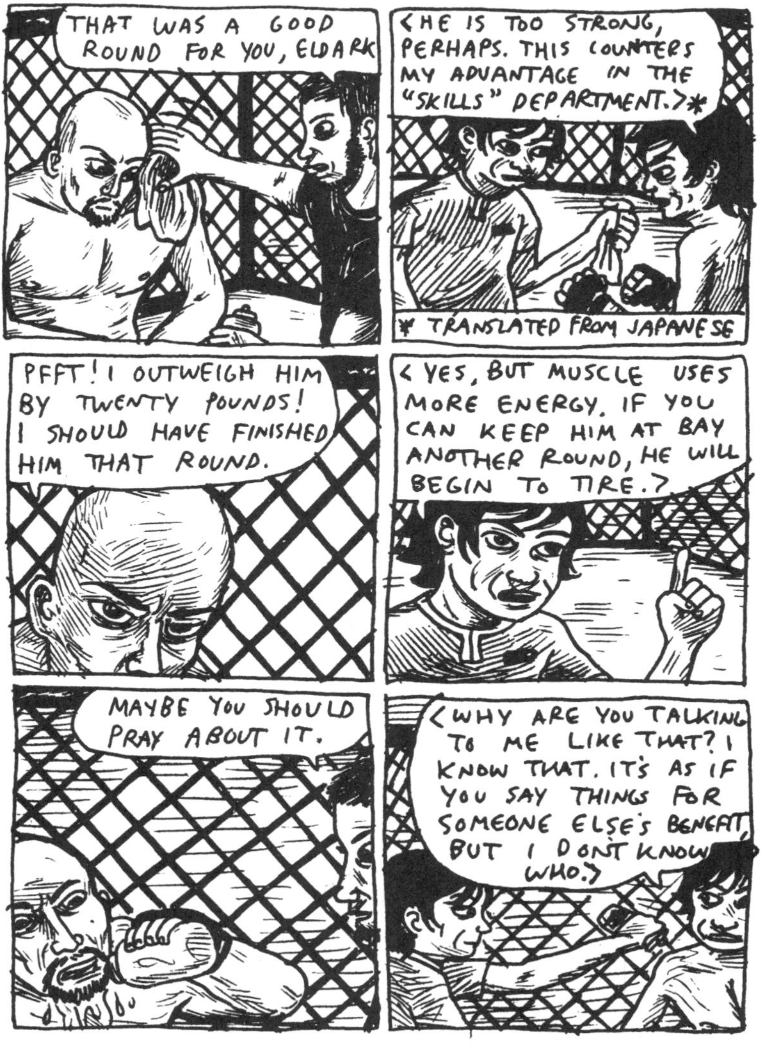
THAT WAS A GOOD ROUND FOR YOU, ELDARK
<HE IS TOO STRONG, PERHAPS. THIS COUNTERS MY ADVANTAGE IN THE "SKILLS" DEPARTMENT.>*
* TRANSLATED FROM JAPANESE
PFFT! I OUTWEIGH HIM BY TWENTY POUNDS! I SHOULD HAVE FINISHED HIM THAT ROUND.
<YES, BUT MUSCLE USES MORE ENERGY. IF YOU CAN KEEP HIM AT BAY ANOTHER ROUND, HE WILL BEGIN TO TIRE.>
MAYBE YOU SHOULD PRAY ABOUT IT.
<WHY ARE YOU TALKING TO ME LIKE THAT? I KNOW THAT. IT'S AS IF YOU SAY THINGS FOR SOMEONE ELSE'S BENEFIT, BUT I DON'T KNOW WHO.>

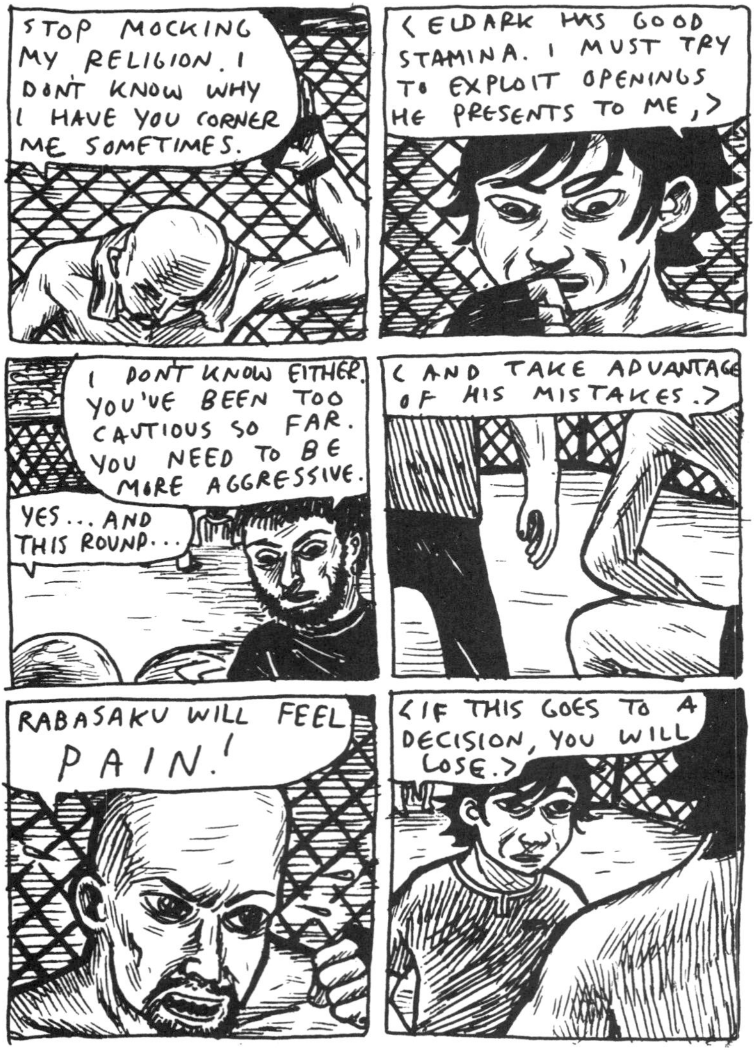
STOP MOCKING MY RELIGION. I DON'T KNOW WHY I HAVE YOU CORNER ME SOMETIMES.
<ELDARK HAS GOOD STAMINA. I MUST TRY TO EXPLOIT OPENINGS HE PRESENTS TO ME,>
I DONT KNOW EITHER. YOU'VE BEEN TOO CAUTIOUS SO FAR. YOU NEED TO BE MORE AGGRESSIVE.
YES... AND THIS ROUND...
<AND TAKE ADVANTAGE OF HIS MISTAKES.>
RABASAKU WILL FEEL PAIN!
<IF THIS GOES TO A DECISION, YOU WILL LOSE.>

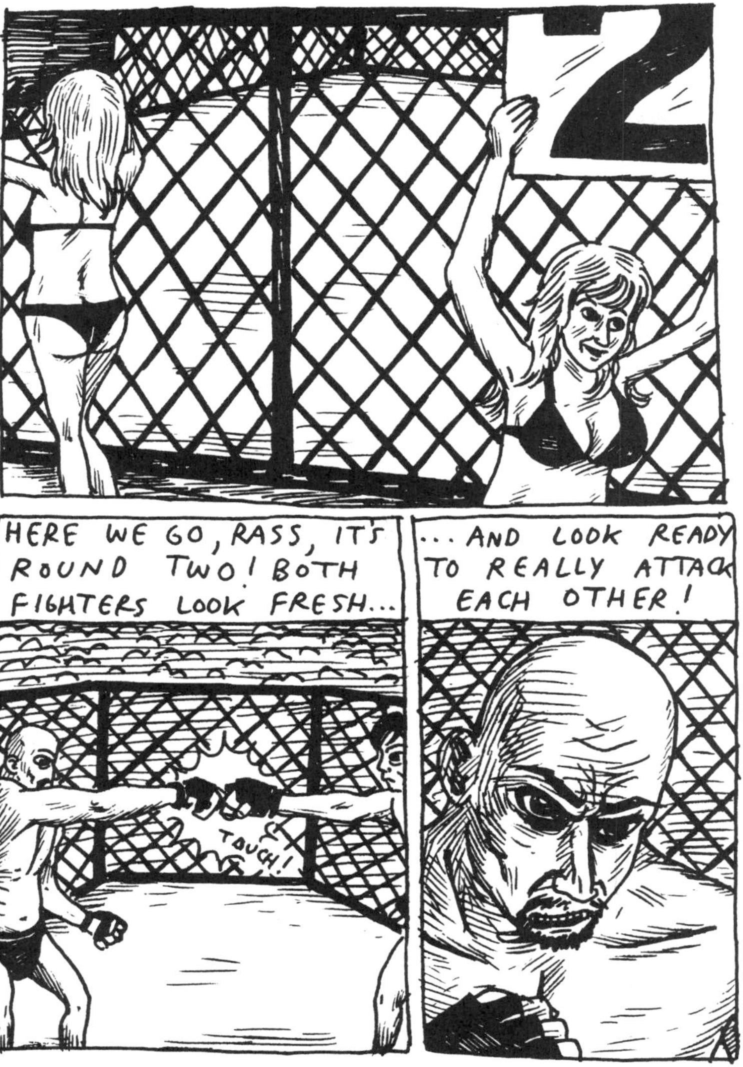
2
HERE WE GO, RASS, IT'S ROUND TWO! BOTH FIGHTERS LOOK FRESH...
TOUCH!
...AND LOOK READY TO REALLY ATTACK EACH OTHER!

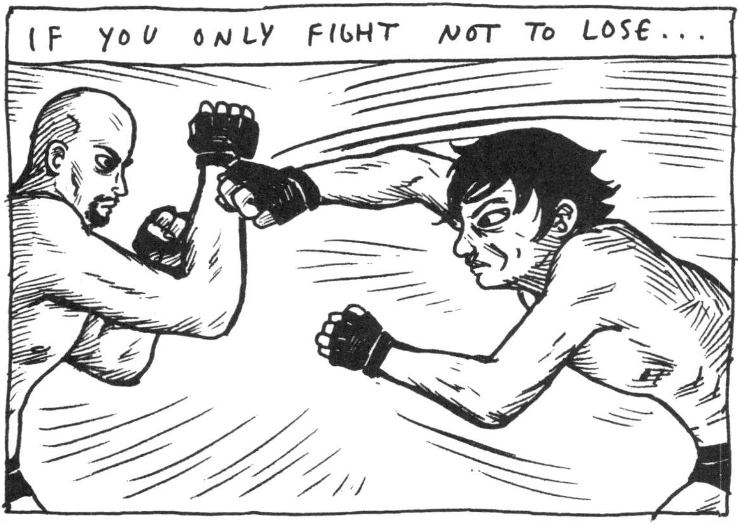
IF YOU ONLY FIGHT NOT TO LOSE...

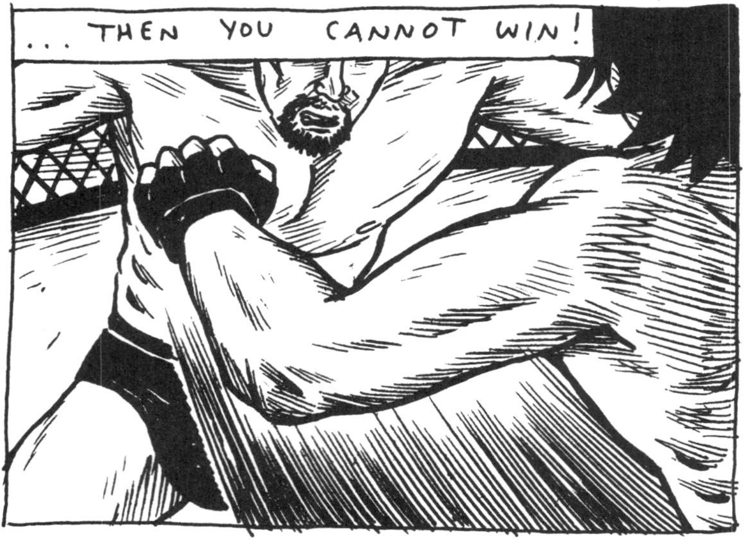
...THEN YOU CANNOT WIN!

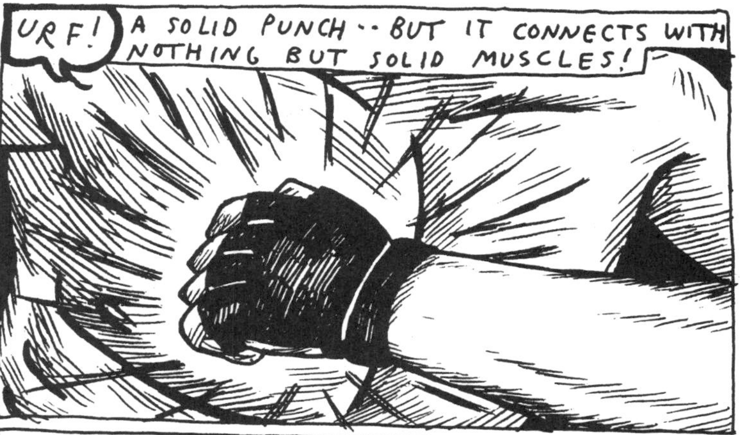
URF!
A SOLID PUNCH.. BUT IT CONNECTS WITH NOTHING BUT SOLID MUSCLES!

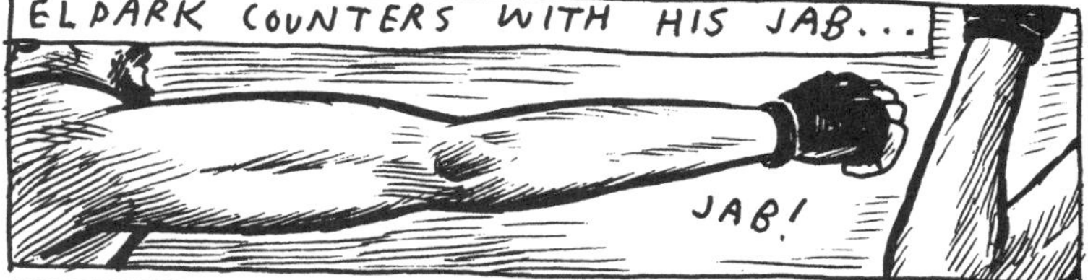
ELDARK COUNTERS WITH HIS JAB...
JAB!

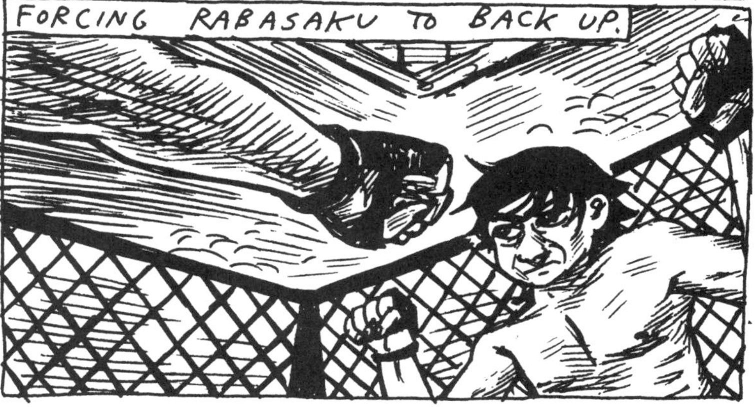
FORCING RABASAKU TO BACK UP.

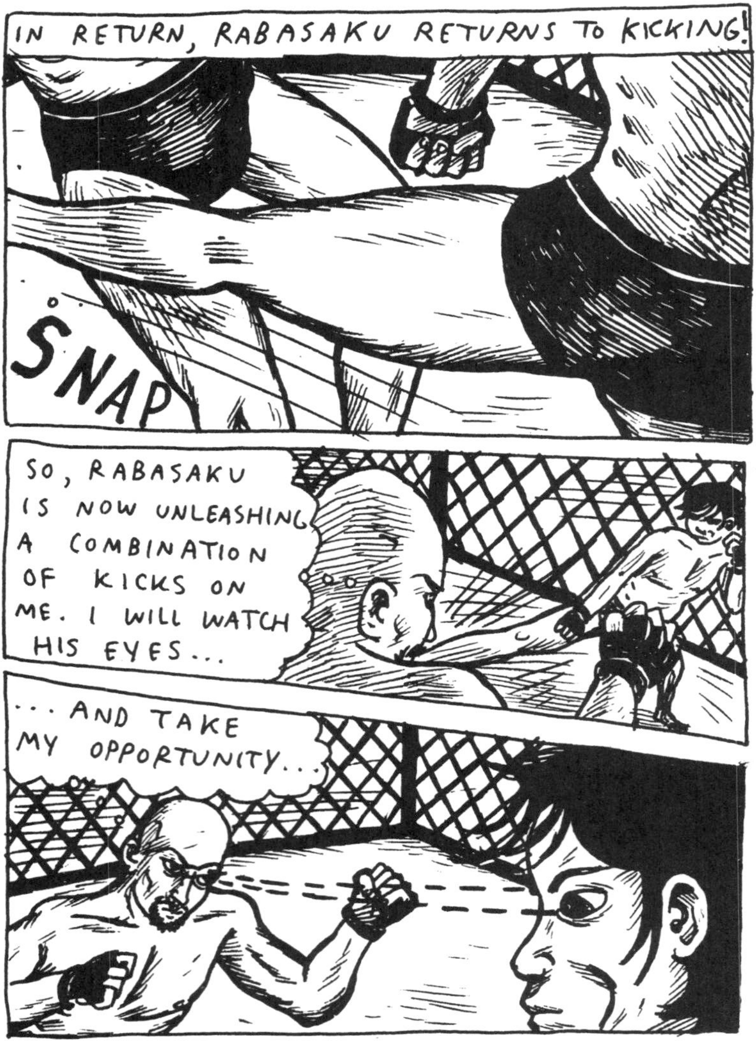
IN RETURN, RABASAKU RETURNS TO KICKING!
SNAP
SO, RABASAKU IS NOW UNLEASHING A COMBINATION OF KICKS ON ME. I WILL WATCH HIS EYES...
...AND TAKE MY OPPORTUNITY...

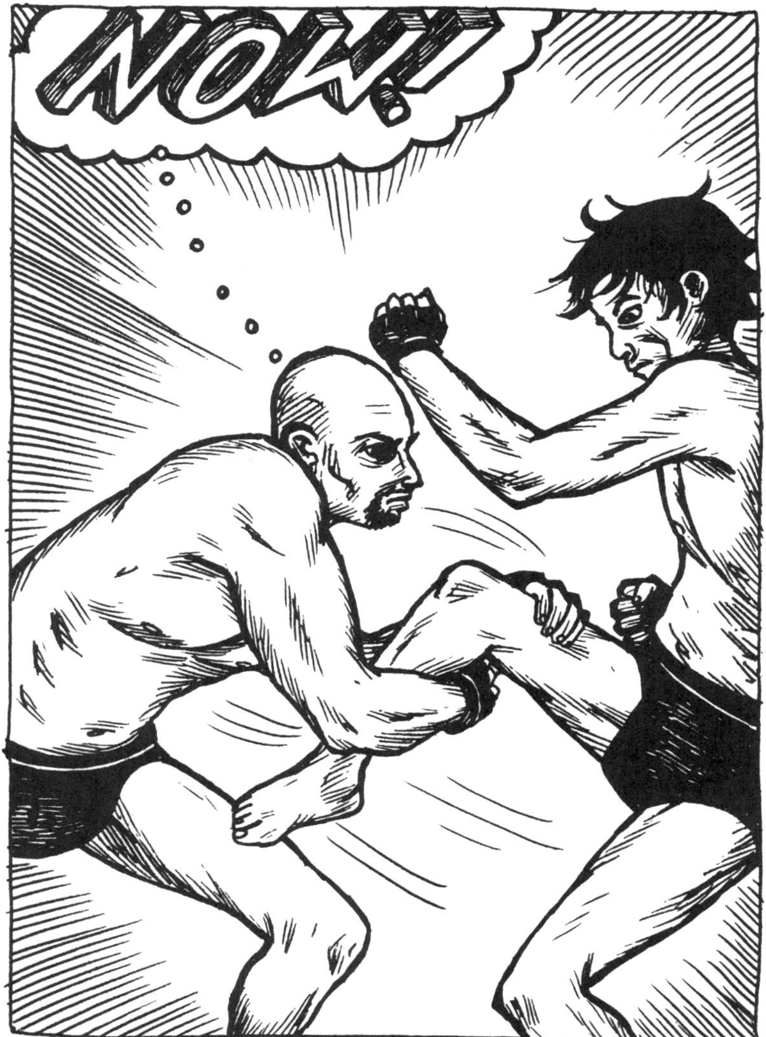
NOW!!

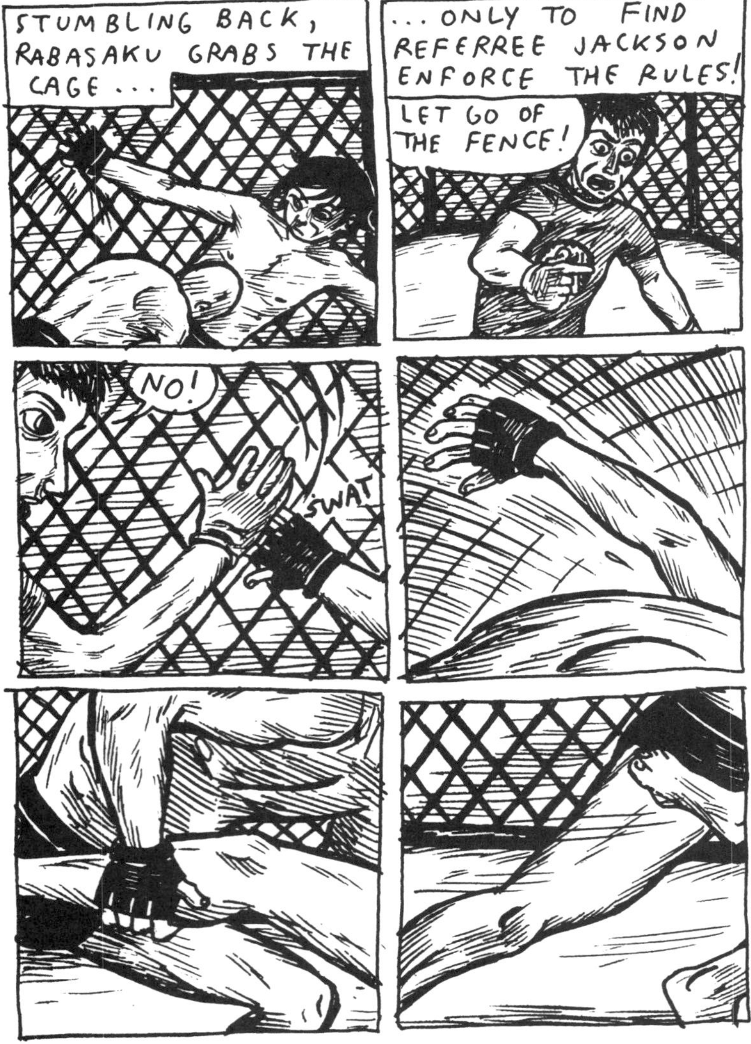
STUMBLING BACK, RABASAKU GRABS THE CAGE...
...ONLY TO FIND REFERREE JACKSON ENFORCE THE RULES!
LET GO OF THE FENCE!
NO!
SWAT

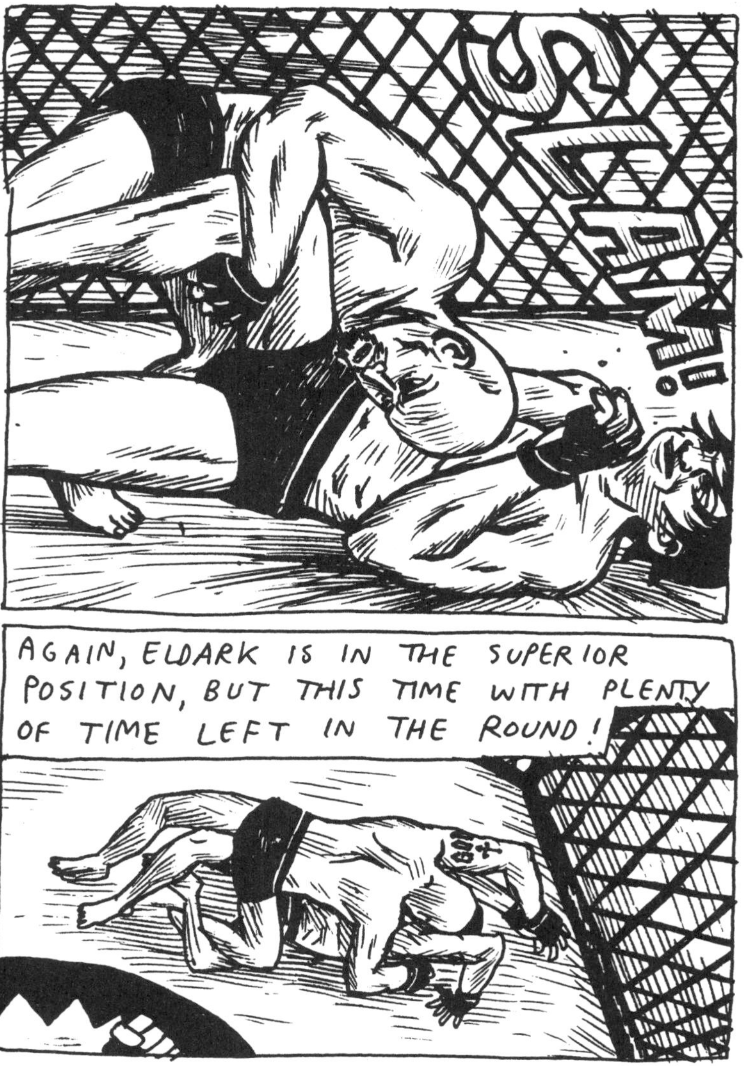
SLAM!!
AGAIN, ELDARK IS IN THE SUPERIOR POSITION, BUT THIS TIME WITH PLENTY OF TIME LEFT IN THE ROUND!

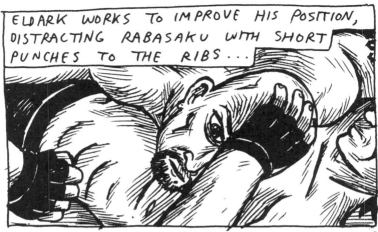

ELDARK WORKS TO IMPROVE HIS POSITION, DISTRACTING RABASAKU WITH SHORT PUNCHES TO THE RIBS...

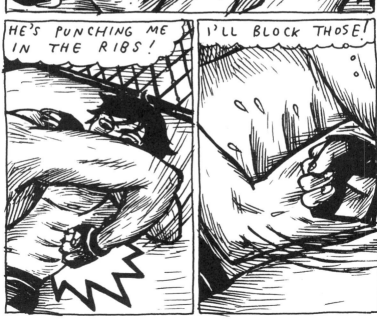

HE'S PUNCHING ME IN THE RIBS!

I'LL BLOCK THOSE!

HA! JUST AS I PLANNED! WHILE YOU WERE DISTRACTED BY VIRTUALLY HARMLESS, ANNOYING BODY PUNCHES, I MOVED INTO AN EVEN MORE DOMINANT POSITION!
GASP!

NOW I CAN UTILIZE YET ANOTHER OF MY DEVASTATING STRIKES!

THE ELBOW!

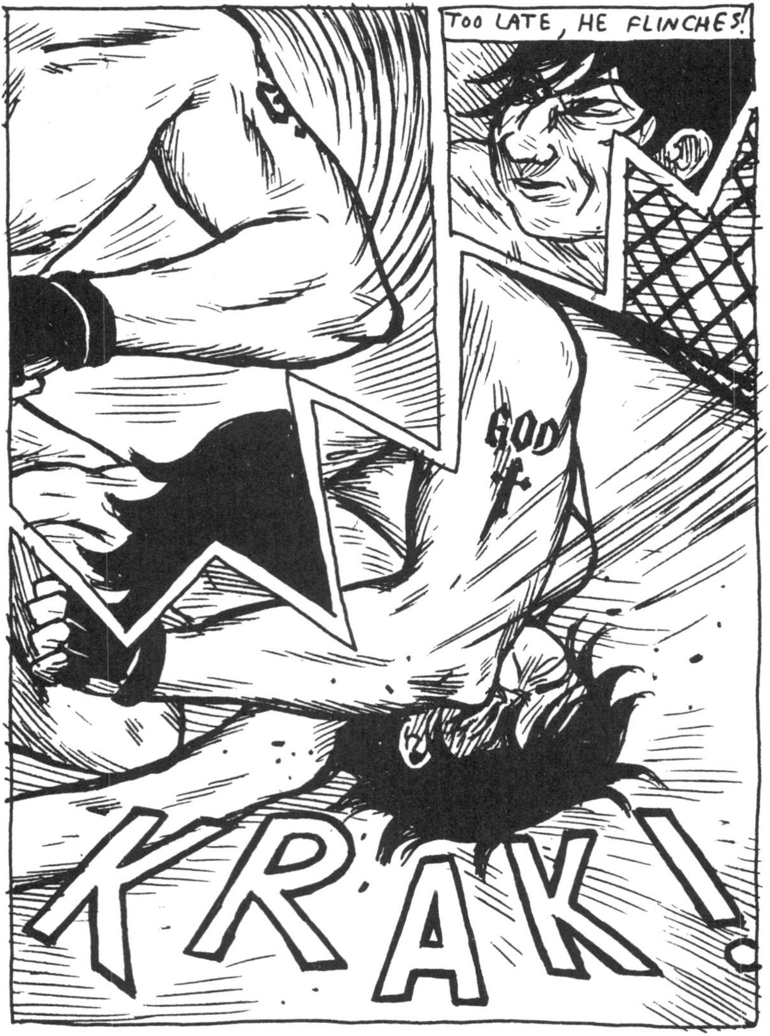
TOO LATE, HE FLINCHES!
GOD
KRAK!

SOON, BLOOD IS POURING FROM THE CUT NEAR RABASAKU'S EYE --

"MASSIVE AMOUNTS OF BLOOD!"

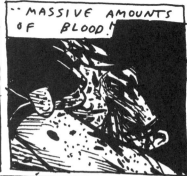

REFERREE JACKSON STEPS IN AGAIN TO BREAK APART THE FIGHTERS...

AND CALLS IN THE CAGE DOCTOR!

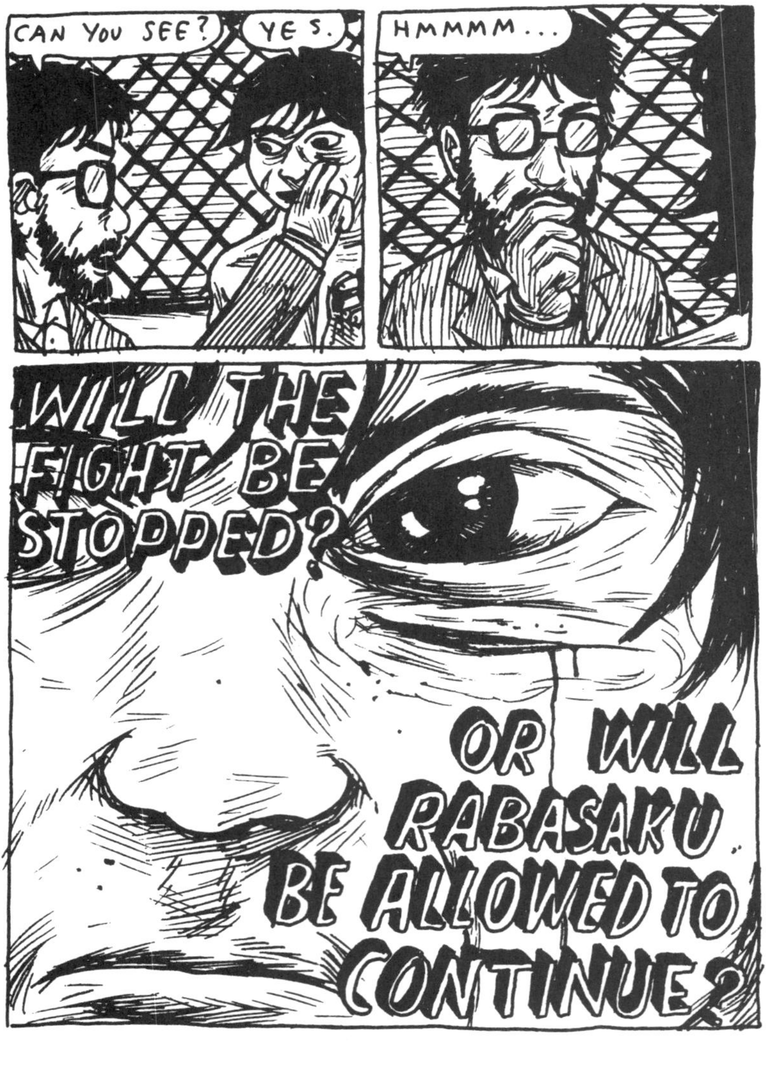

CAN YOU SEE?
YES.
HMMMM...
WILL THE FIGHT BE STOPPED?
OR WILL RABASAKU BE ALLOWED TO CONTINUE?

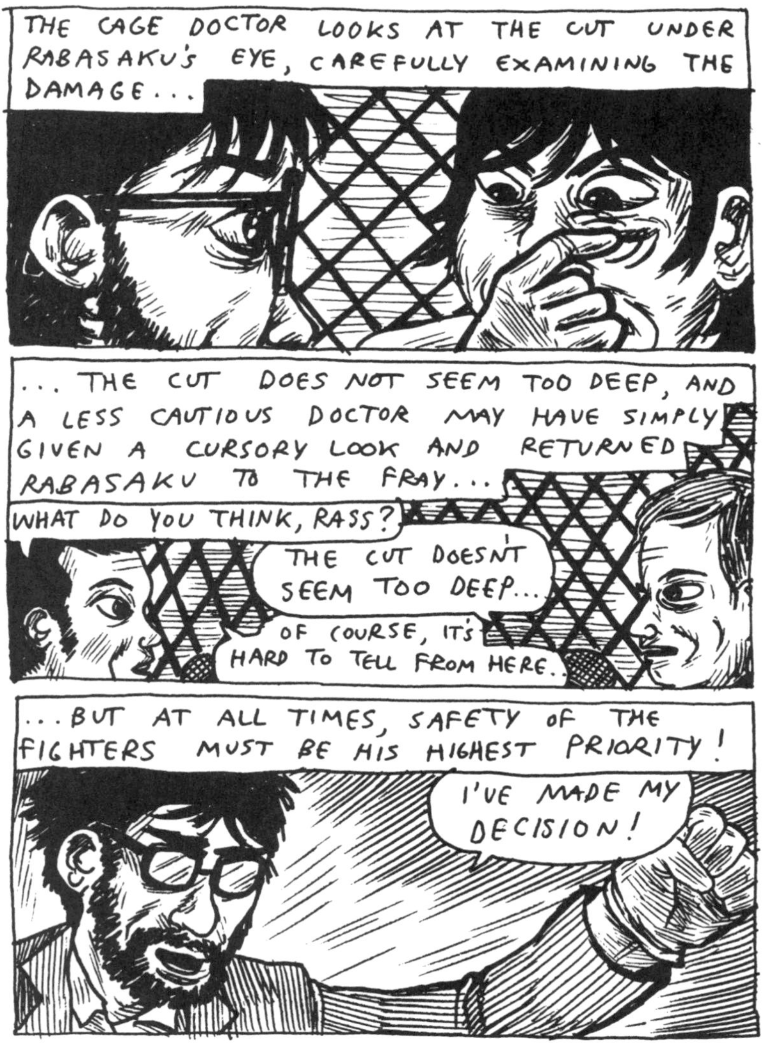
THE CAGE DOCTOR LOOKS AT THE CUT UNDER RABASAKU'S EYE, CAREFULLY EXAMINING THE DAMAGE...
...THE CUT DOES NOT SEEM TOO DEEP, AND A LESS CAUTIOUS DOCTOR MAY HAVE SIMPLY GIVEN A CURSORY LOOK AND RETURNED RABASAKU TO THE FRAY...
WHAT DO YOU THINK, RASS?
THE CUT DOESN'T SEEM TOO DEEP...
OF COURSE, IT'S HARD TO TELL FROM HERE...
...BUT AT ALL TIMES, SAFETY OF THE FIGHTERS MUST BE HIS HIGHEST PRIORITY!
I'VE MADE MY DECISION!

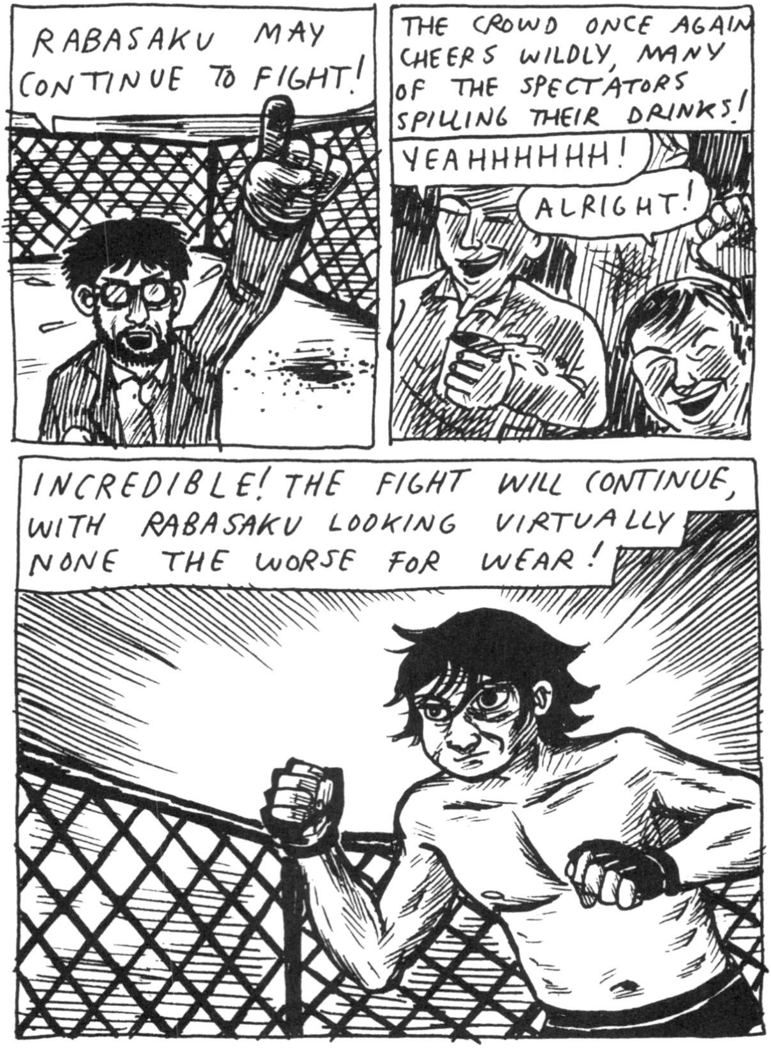
RABASAKU MAY CONTINUE TO FIGHT!
THE CROWD ONCE AGAIN CHEERS WILDLY, MANY OF THE SPECTATORS SPILLING THEIR DRINKS!
YEAHHHHHH!
ALRIGHT!
INCREDIBLE! THE FIGHT WILL CONTINUE, WITH RABASAKU LOOKING VIRTUALLY NONE THE WORSE FOR WEAR!

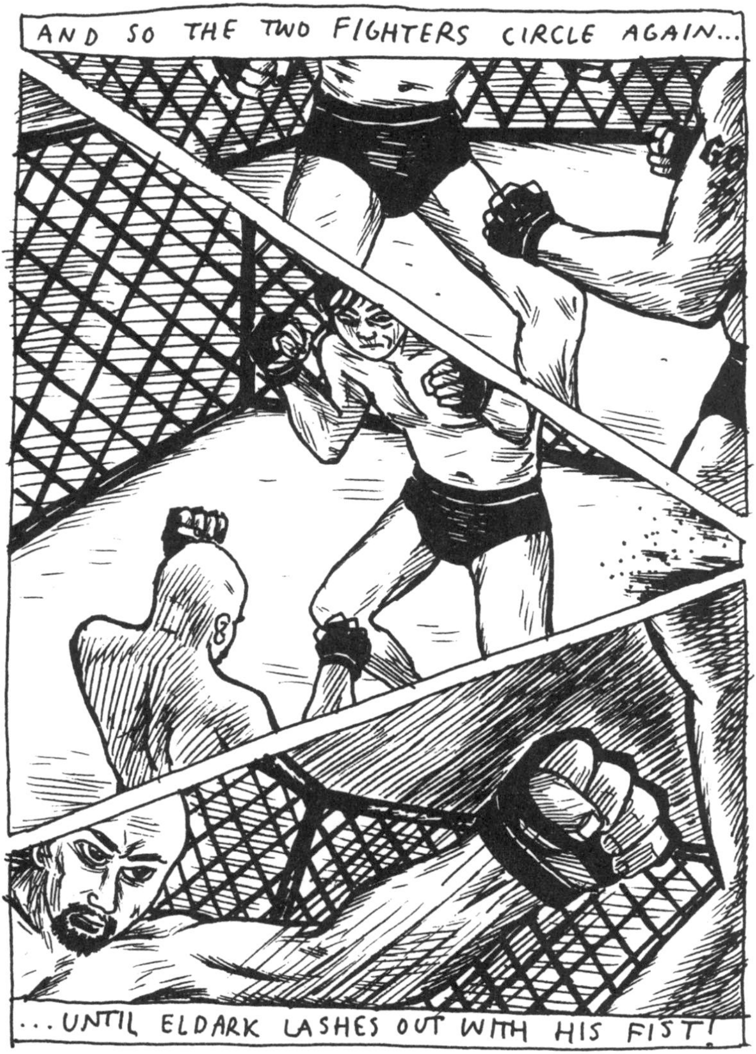
AND SO THE TWO FIGHTERS CIRCLE AGAIN...
...UNTIL ELDARK LASHES OUT WITH HIS FIST!

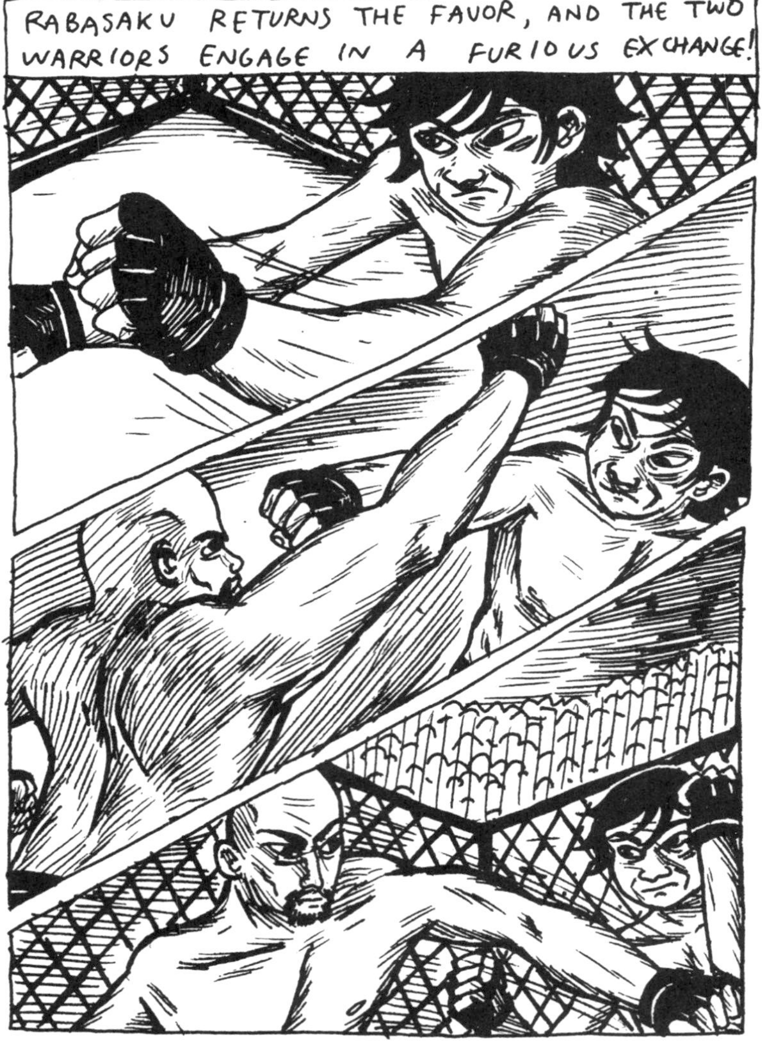
RABASAKU RETURNS THE FAVOR, AND THE TWO WARRIORS ENGAGE IN A FURIOUS EXCHANGE!

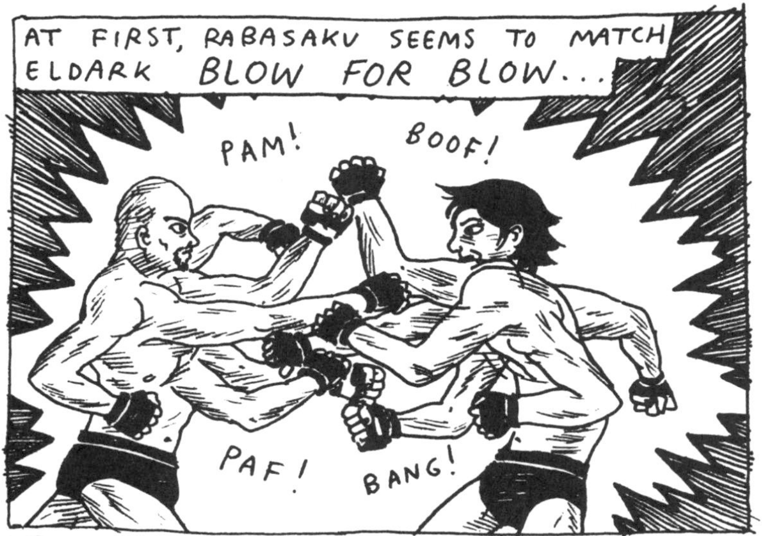
AT FIRST, RABASAKU SEEMS TO MATCH ELDARK BLOW FOR BLOW...
PAM!
BOOF!
PAF!
BANG!

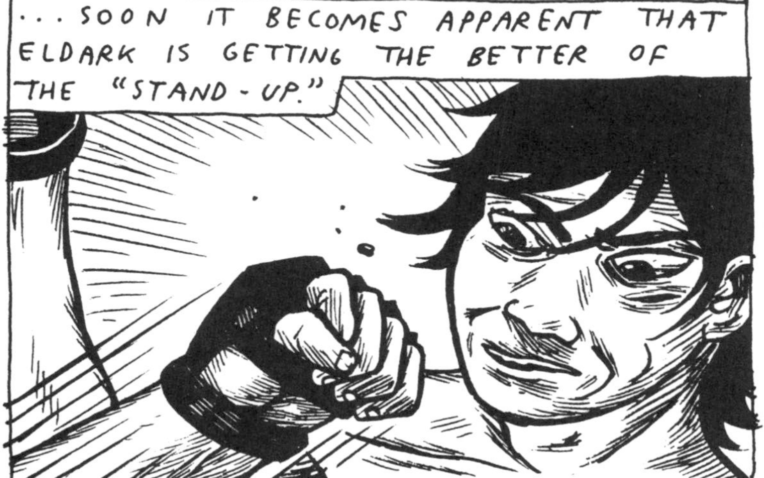
...SOON IT BECOMES APPARENT THAT ELDARK IS GETTING THE BETTER OF THE "STAND-UP."

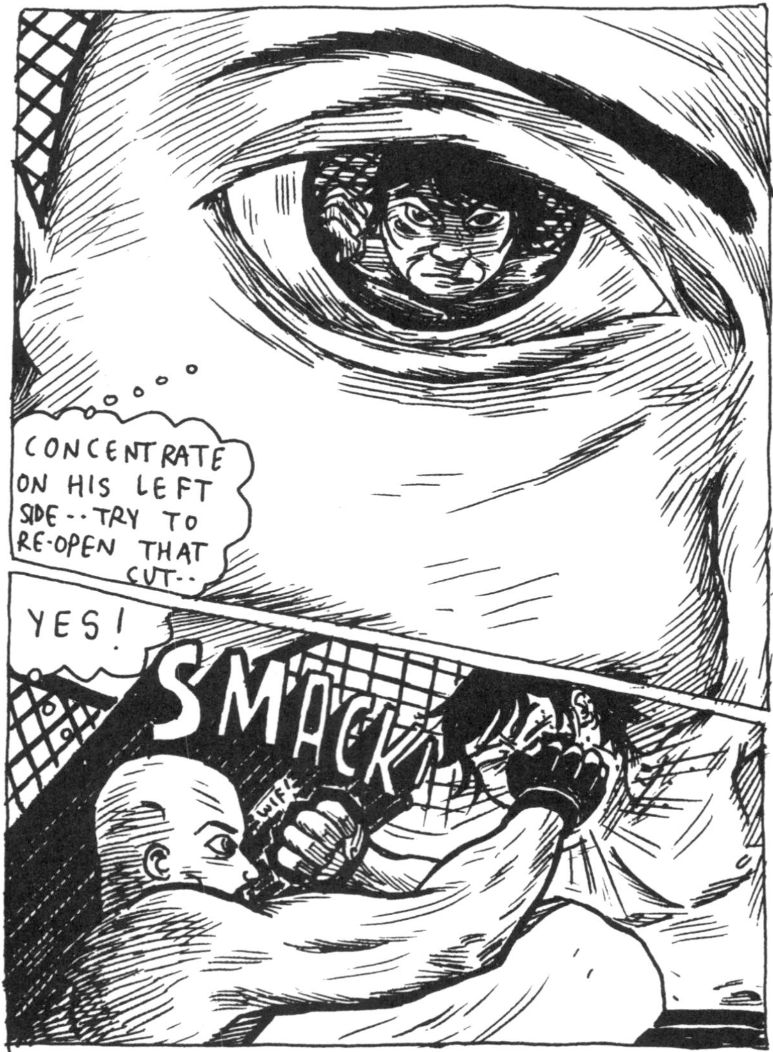
CONCENTRATE ON HIS LEFT SIDE--TRY TO RE-OPEN THAT CUT--
YES!
SMACK

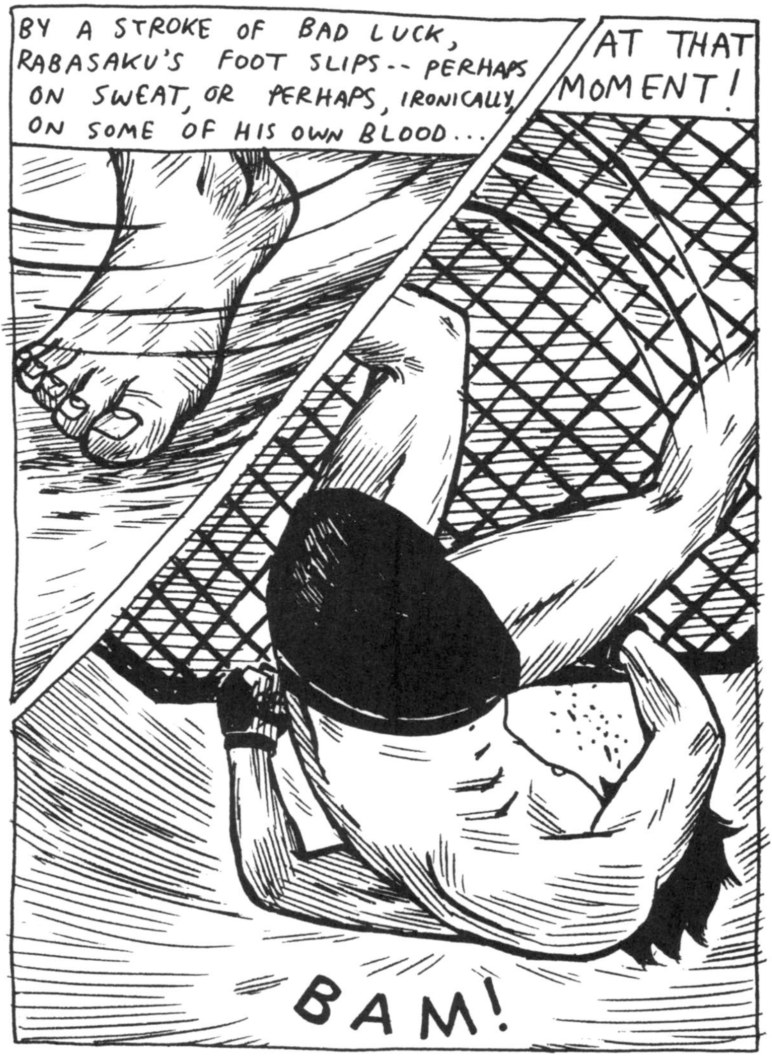
BY A STROKE OF BAD LUCK, RABASAKU'S FOOT SLIPS -- PERHAPS ON SWEAT, OR PERHAPS, IRONICALLY, ON SOME OF HIS OWN BLOOD...
AT THAT MOMENT!
BAM!

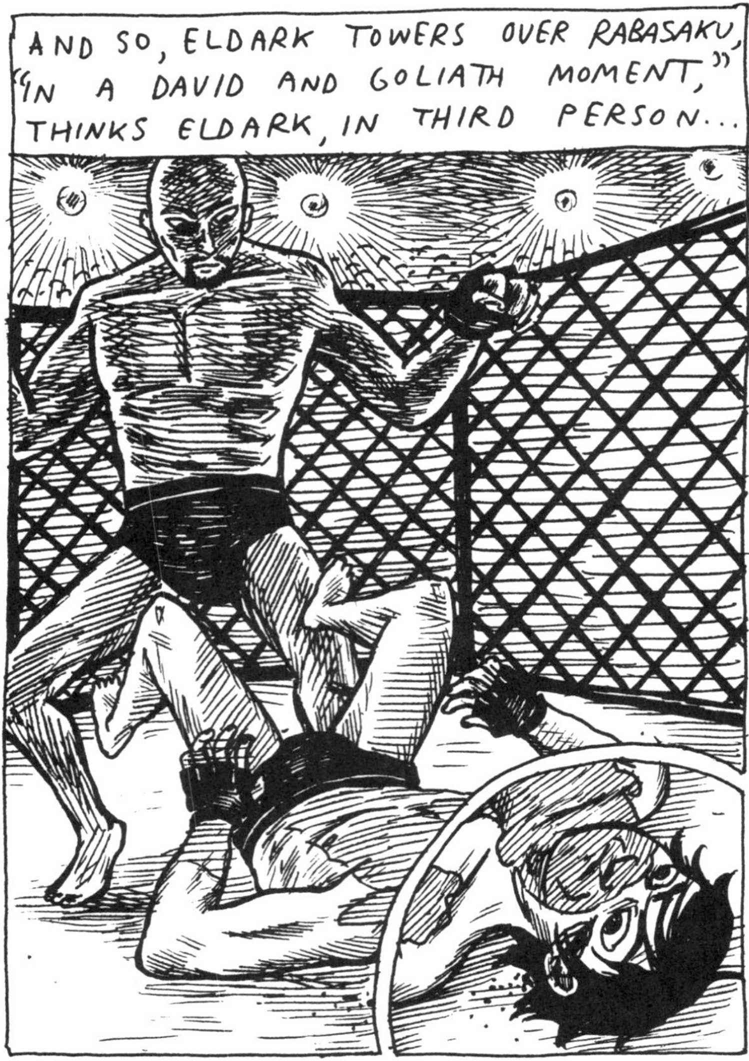
AND SO, ELDARK TOWERS OVER RABASAKU, "IN A DAVID AND GOLIATH MOMENT," THINKS ELDARK, IN THIRD PERSON...

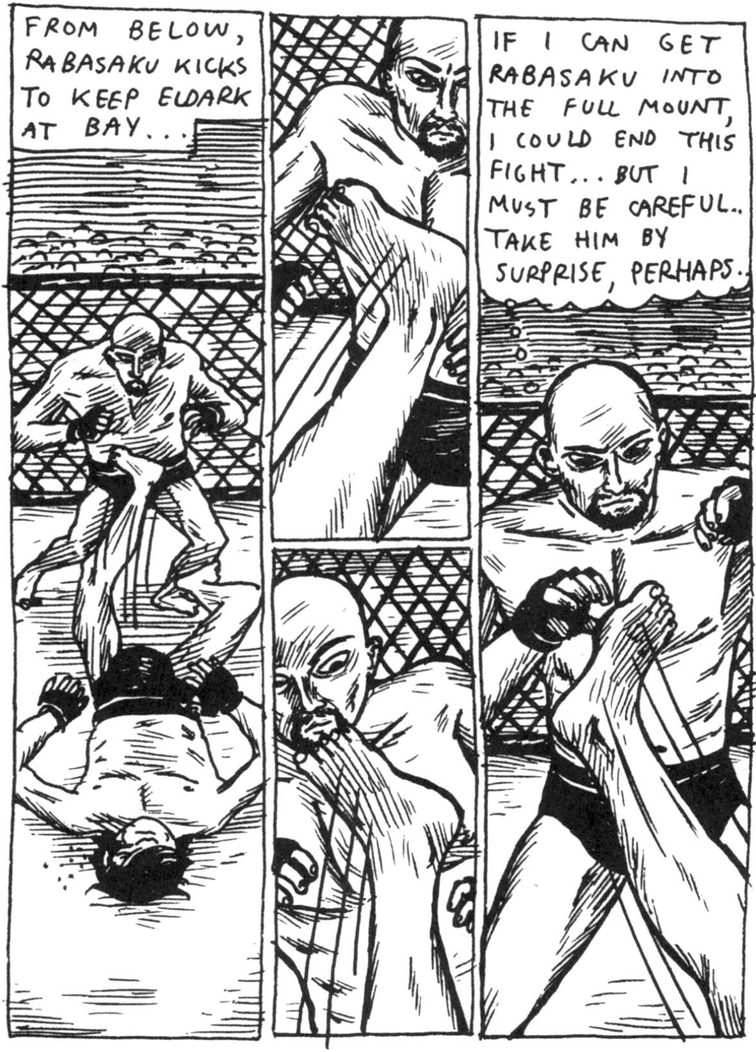
FROM BELOW, RABASAKU KICKS TO KEEP ELDARK AT BAY...
IF I CAN GET RABASAKU INTO THE FULL MOUNT, I COULD END THIS FIGHT... BUT I MUST BE CAREFUL.. TAKE HIM BY SURPRISE, PERHAPS..

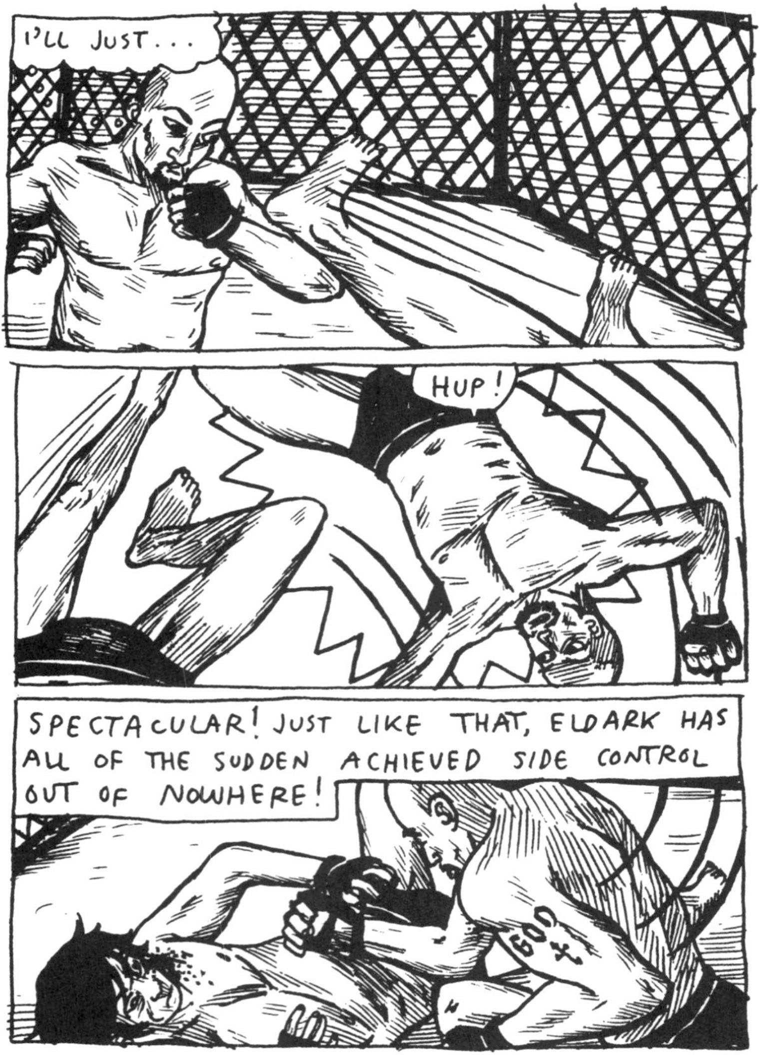
I'LL JUST...
HUP!
SPECTACULAR! JUST LIKE THAT, ELDARK HAS ALL OF THE SUDDEN ACHIEVED SIDE CONTROL OUT OF NOWHERE!

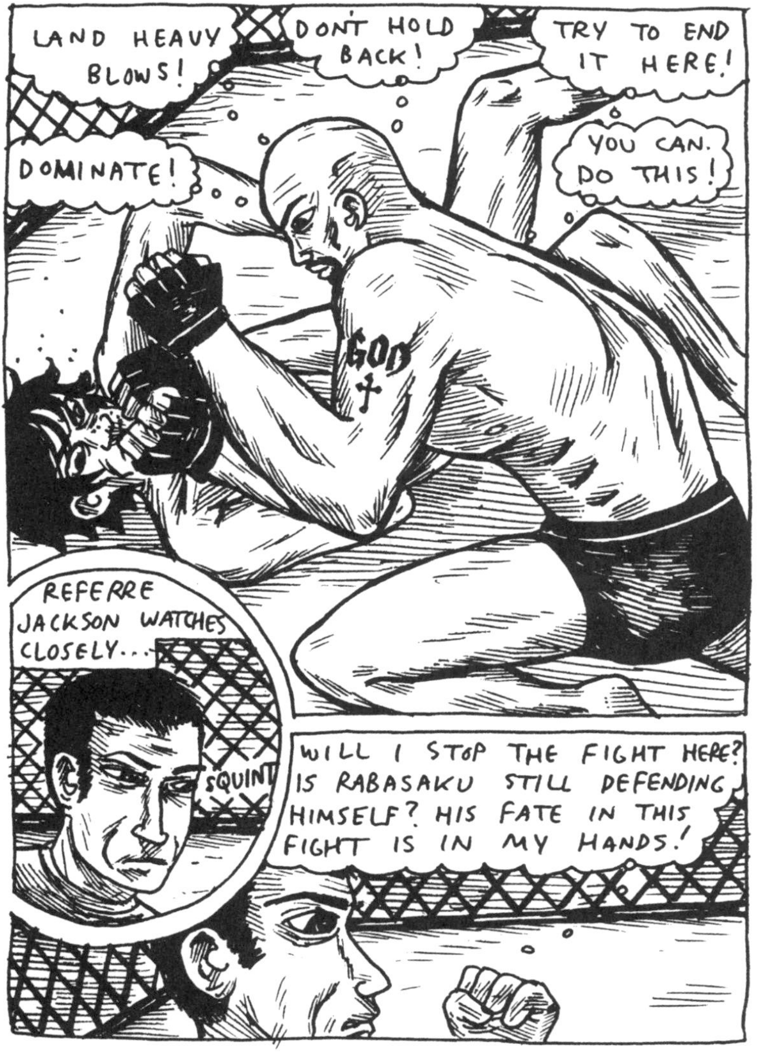
LAND HEAVY BLOWS!
DON'T HOLD BACK!
TRY TO END IT HERE!
DOMINATE!
YOU CAN. DO THIS!
GOD
REFERRE JACKSON WATCHES CLOSELY...
SQUINT
WILL I STOP THE FIGHT HERE? IS RABASAKU STILL DEFENDING HIMSELF? HIS FATE IN THIS FIGHT IS IN MY HANDS!

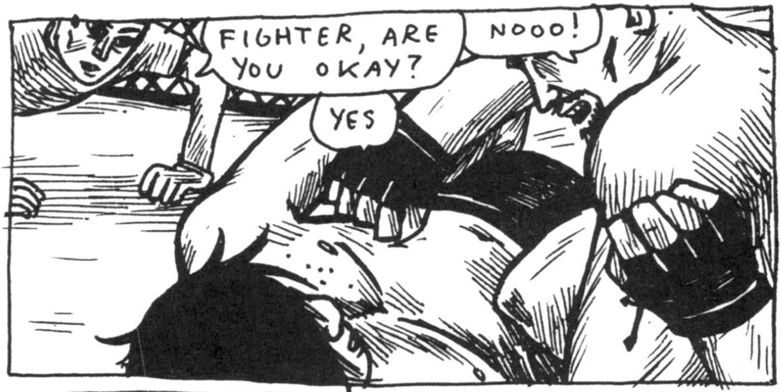
FIGHTER, ARE YOU OKAY?
NOOO!
YES

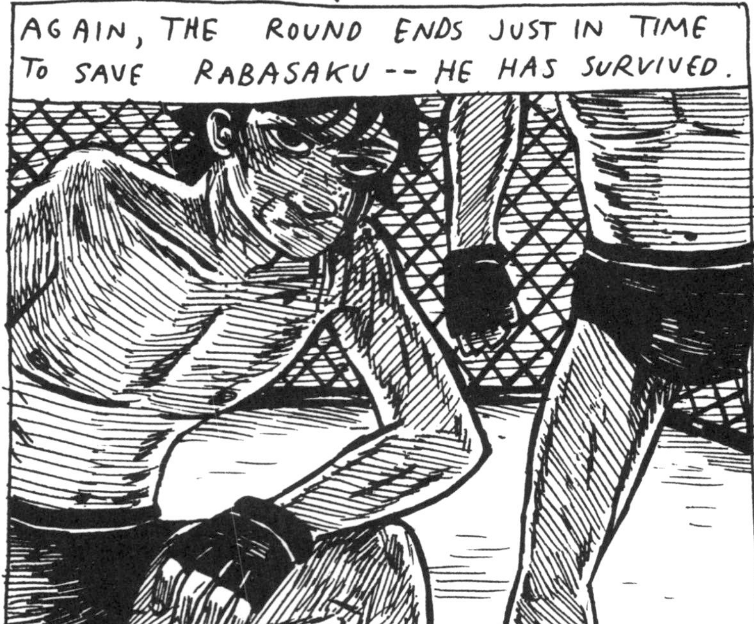
AGAIN, THE ROUND ENDS JUST IN TIME TO SAVE RABASAKU -- HE HAS SURVIVED.

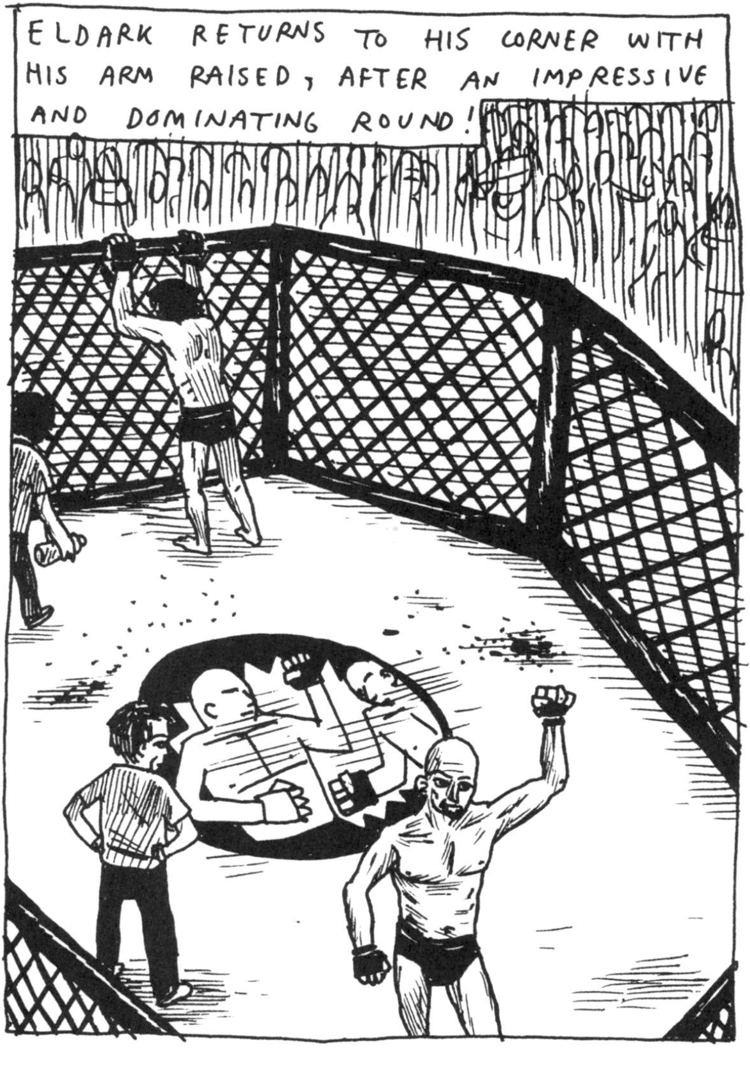
ELDARK RETURNS TO HIS CORNER WITH HIS ARM RAISED, AFTER AN IMPRESSIVE AND DOMINATING ROUND!

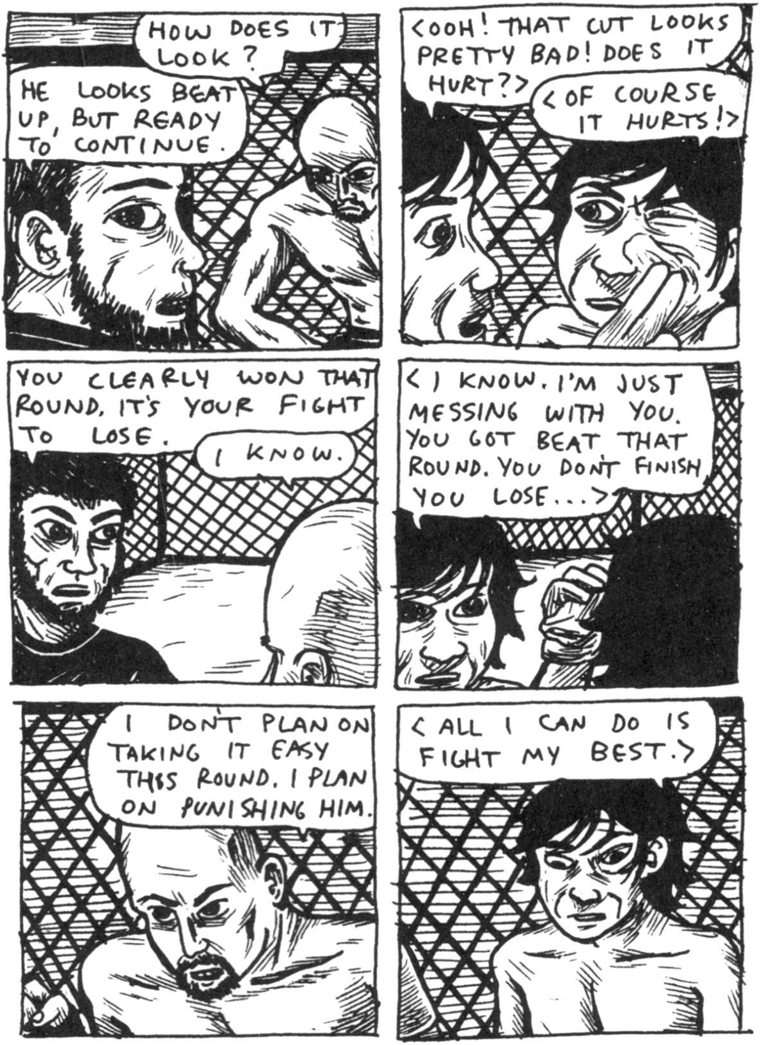
HOW DOES IT LOOK?
HE LOOKS BEAT UP, BUT READY TO CONTINUE.
<OOH! THAT CUT LOOKS PRETTY BAD! DOES IT HURT?>
<OF COURSE IT HURTS!>
YOU CLEARLY WON THAT ROUND. IT'S YOUR FIGHT TO LOSE.
I KNOW.
<I KNOW. I'M JUST MESSING WITH YOU. YOU GOT BEAT THAT ROUND. YOU DON'T FINISH YOU LOSE...>
I DON'T PLAN ON TAKING IT EASY THIS ROUND. I PLAN ON PUNISHING HIM.
<ALL I CAN DO IS FIGHT MY BEST.>

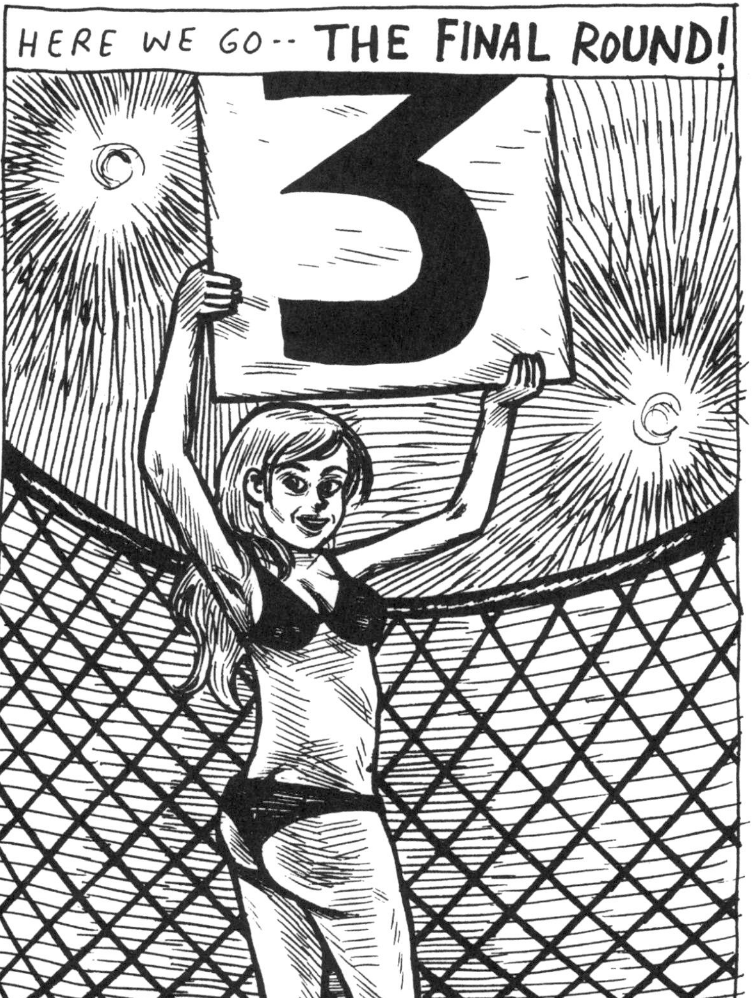
HERE WE GO-- THE FINAL ROUND!
3

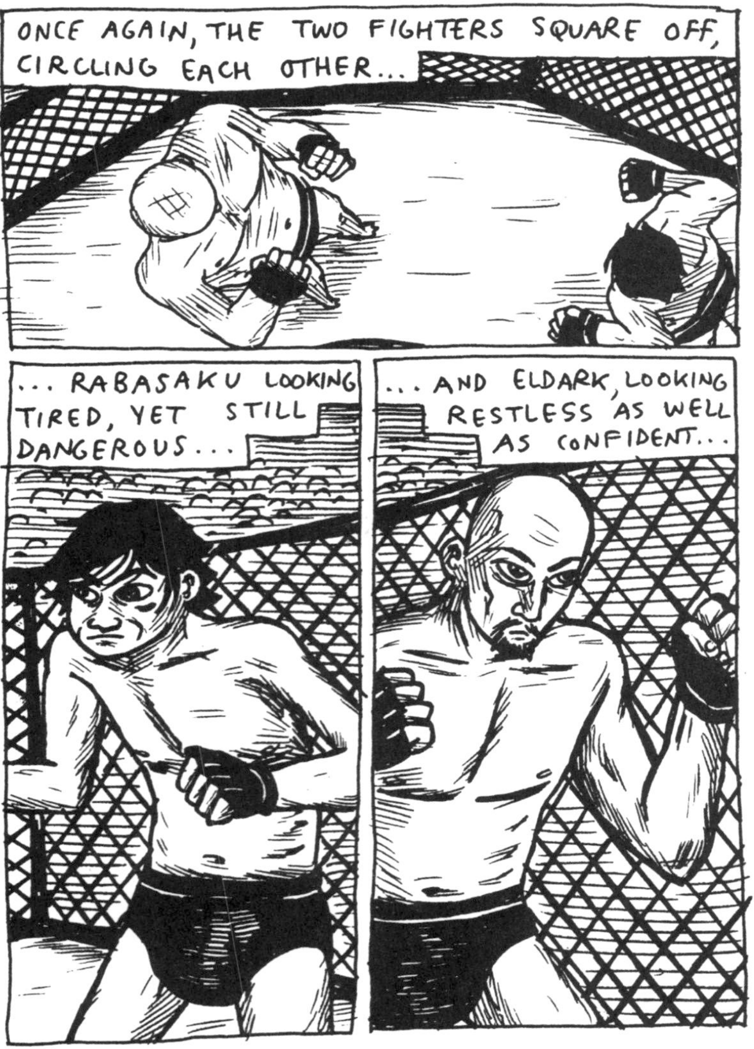
ONCE AGAIN, THE TWO FIGHTERS SQUARE OFF, CIRCLING EACH OTHER...
... RABASAKU LOOKING TIRED, YET STILL DANGEROUS...
... AND ELDARK, LOOKING RESTLESS AS WELL AS CONFIDENT...

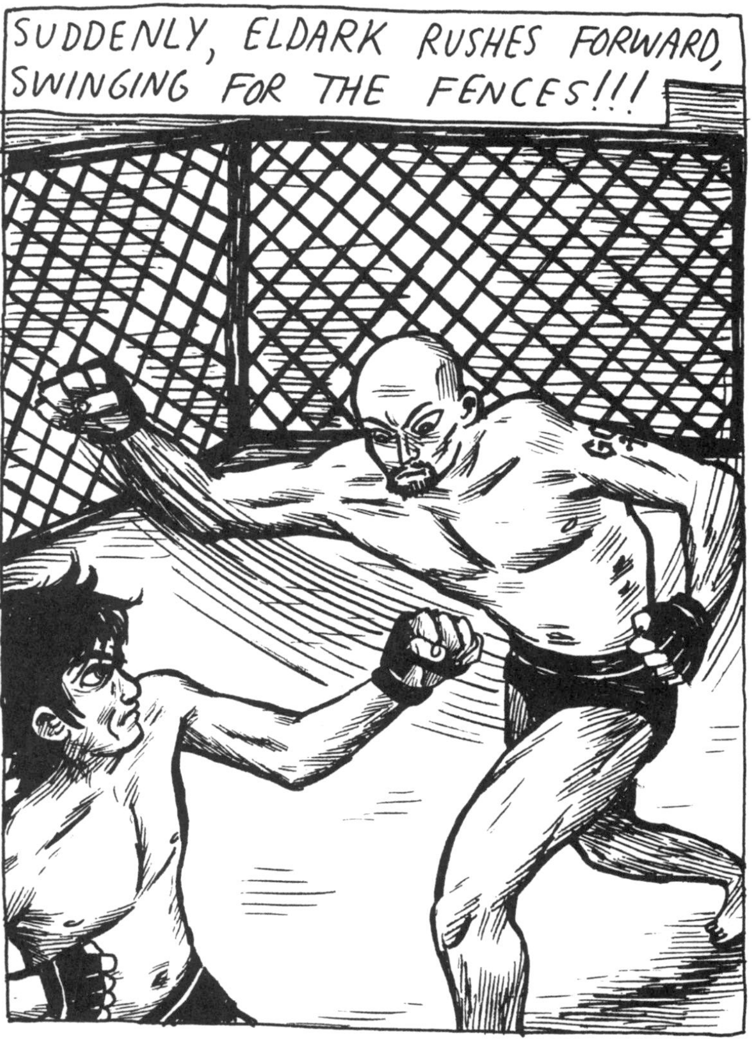
SUDDENLY, ELDARK RUSHES FORWARD, SWINGING FOR THE FENCES!!!

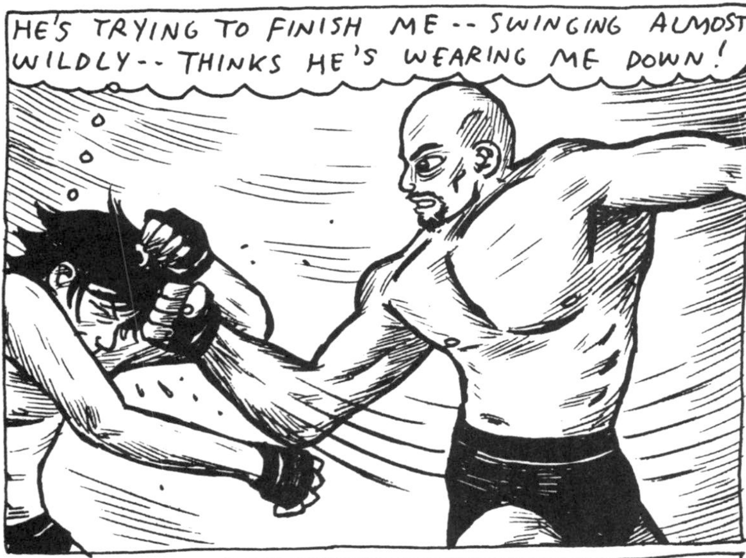
HE'S TRYING TO FINISH ME -- SWINGING ALMOST WILDLY -- THINKS HE'S WEARING ME DOWN!

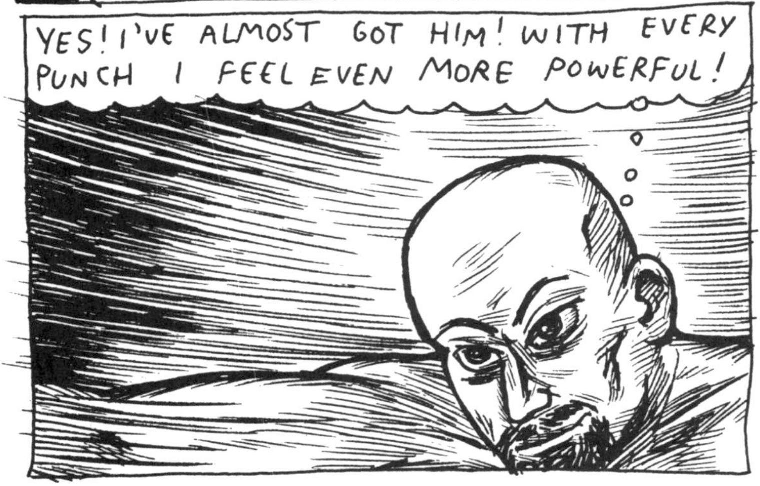
YES! I'VE ALMOST GOT HIM! WITH EVERY PUNCH I FEEL EVEN MORE POWERFUL!

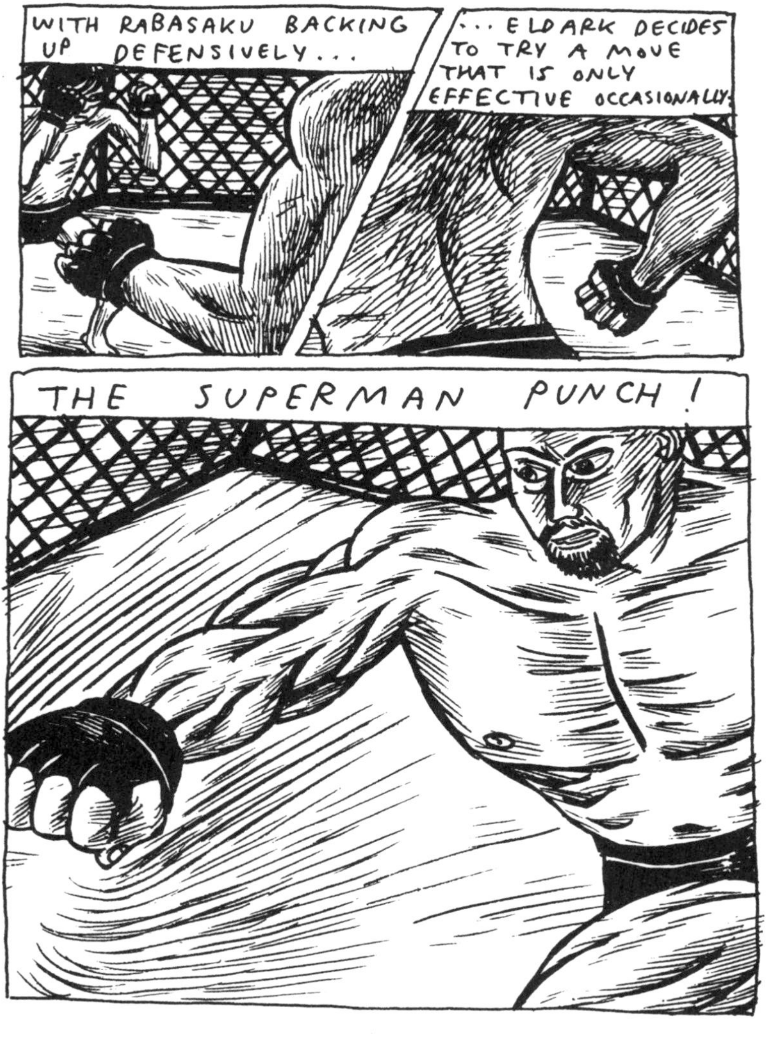
WITH RABASAKU BACKING UP DEFENSIVELY...
...ELDARK DECIDES TO TRY A MOVE THAT IS ONLY EFFECTIVE OCCASIONALLY:
THE SUPERMAN PUNCH!

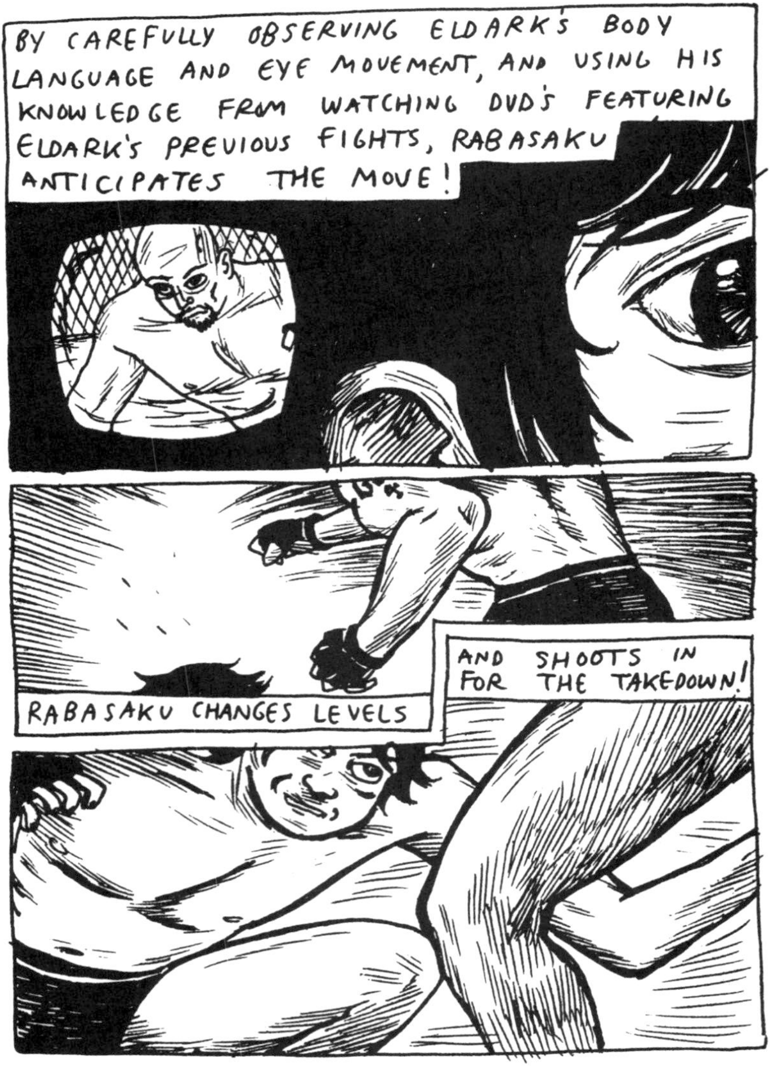
BY CAREFULLY OBSERVING ELDARK'S BODY LANGUAGE AND EYE MOVEMENT, AND USING HIS KNOWLEDGE FROM WATCHING DVD'S FEATURING ELDARK'S PREVIOUS FIGHTS, RABASAKU ANTICIPATES THE MOVE!
RABASAKU CHANGES LEVELS
AND SHOOTS IN FOR THE TAKEDOWN!

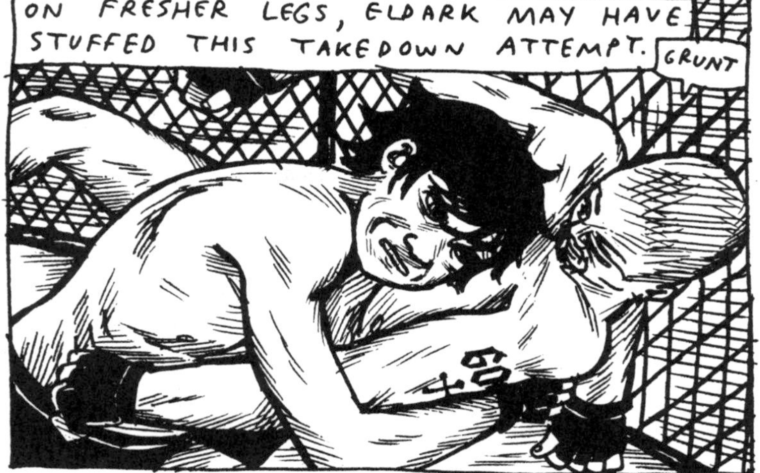
ON FRESHER LEGS, ELDARK MAY HAVE STUFFED THIS TAKEDOWN ATTEMPT.
GRUNT

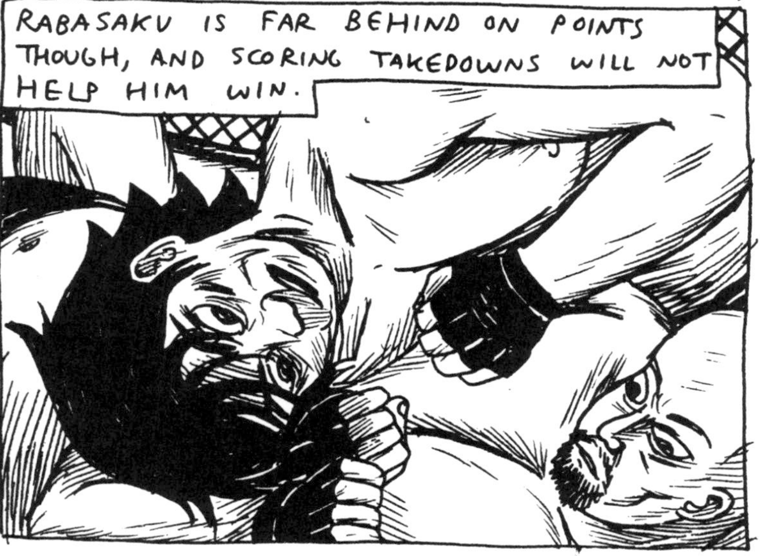
RABASAKU IS FAR BEHIND ON POINTS THOUGH, AND SCORING TAKEDOWNS WILL NOT HELP HIM WIN.

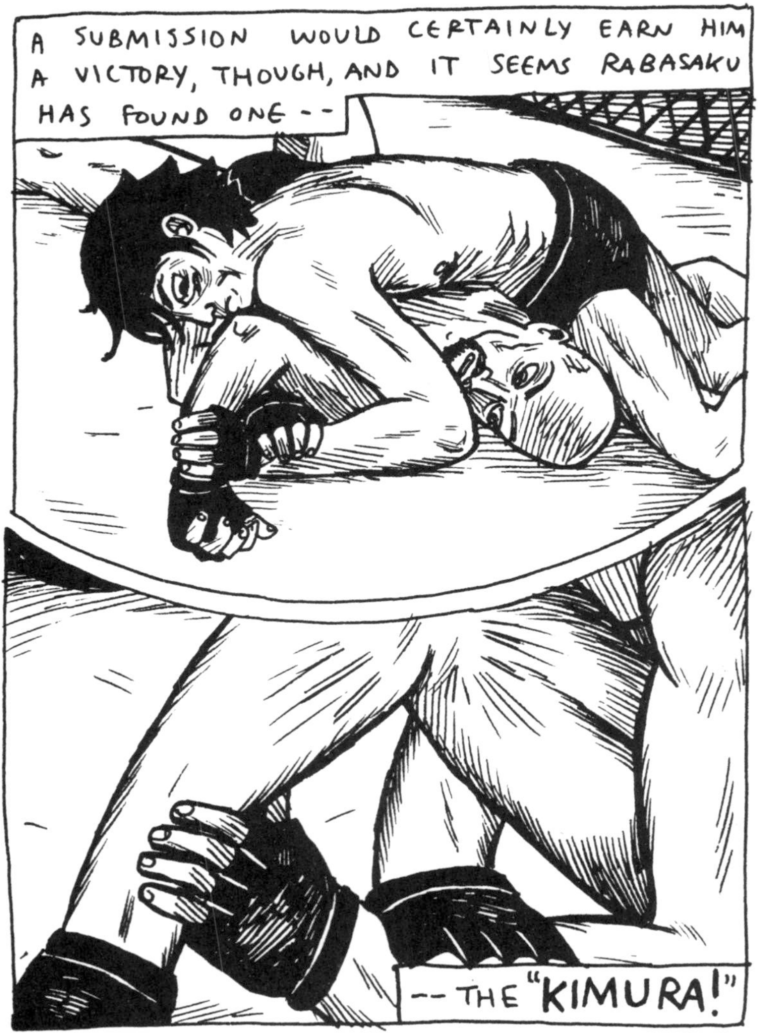
A SUBMISSION WOULD CERTAINLY EARN HIM A VICTORY, THOUGH, AND IT SEEMS RABASAKU HAS FOUND ONE --
-- THE "KIMURA!"

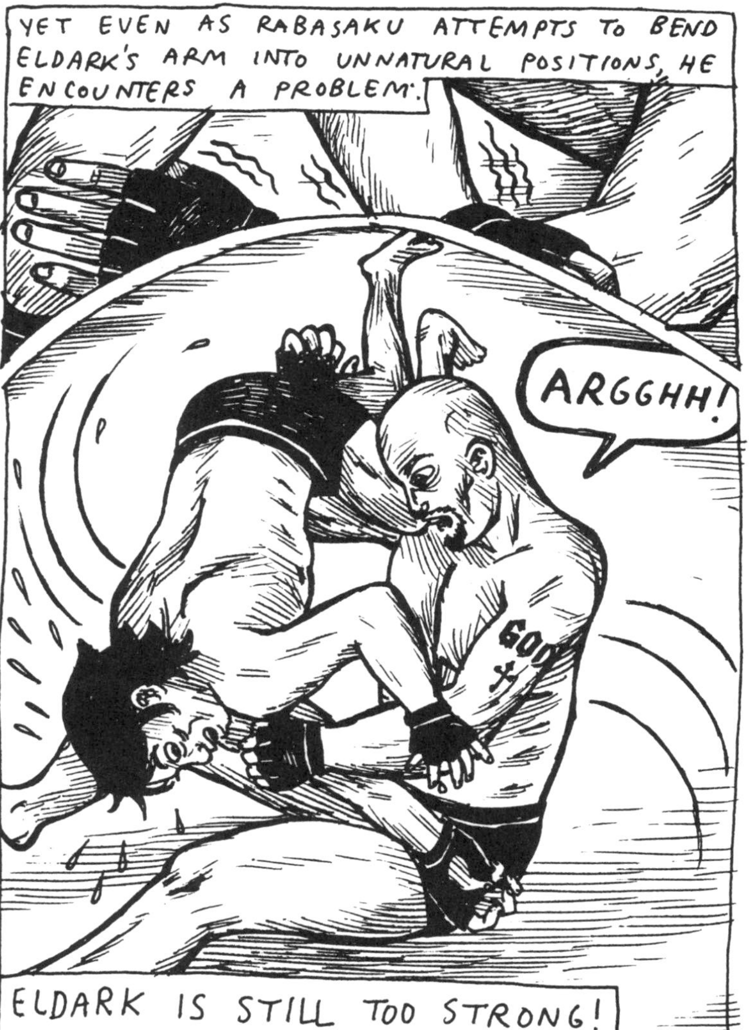
YET EVEN AS RABASAKU ATTEMPTS TO BEND ELDARK'S ARM INTO UNNATURAL POSITIONS, HE ENCOUNTERS A PROBLEM:
ARGGHH!
ELDARK IS STILL TOO STRONG!

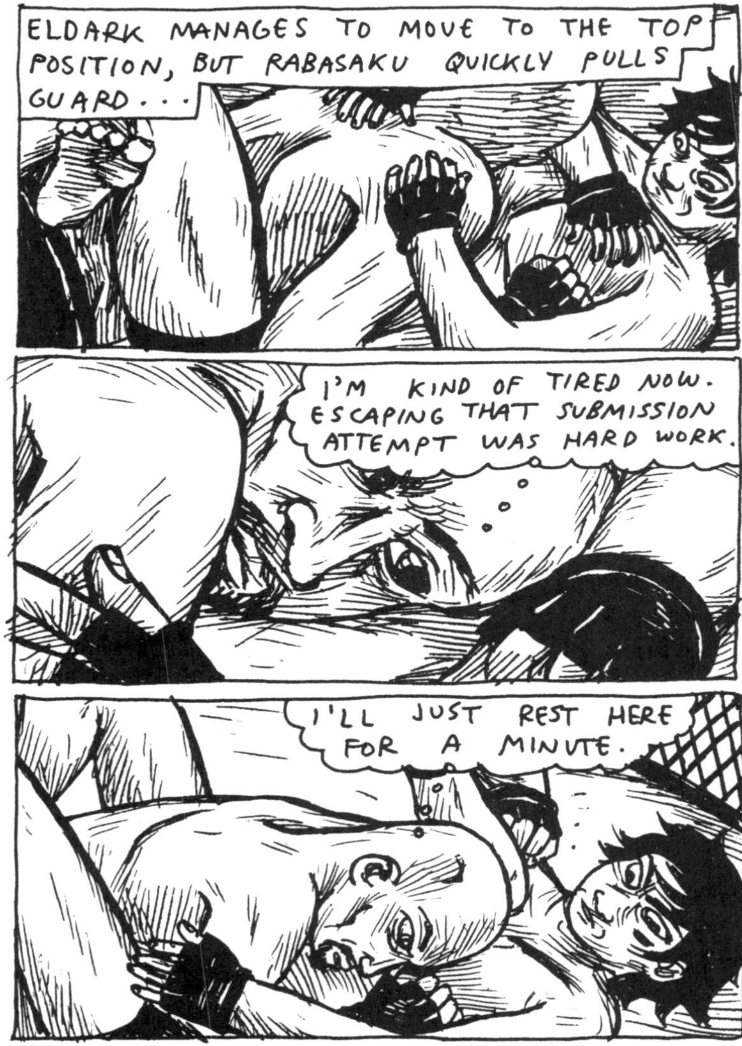
ELDARK MANAGES TO MOVE TO THE TOP POSITION, BUT RABASAKU QUICKLY PULLS GUARD...
I'M KIND OF TIRED NOW. ESCAPING THAT SUBMISSION ATTEMPT WAS HARD WORK.
I'LL JUST REST HERE FOR A MINUTE.

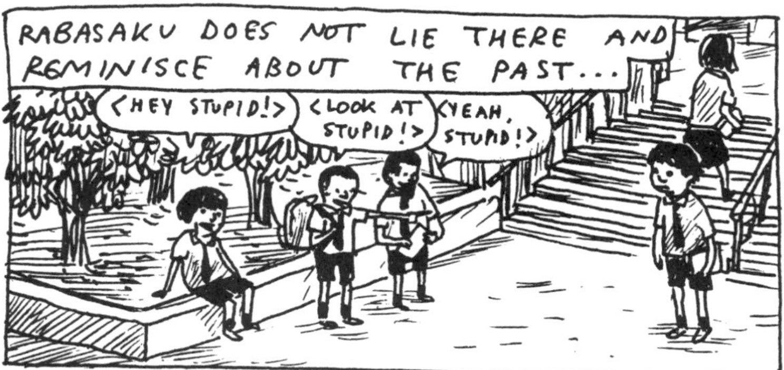
RABASAKU DOES NOT LIE THERE AND REMINISCE ABOUT THE PAST...
<HEY STUPID!>
<LOOK AT STUPID!>
<YEAH, STUPID!>

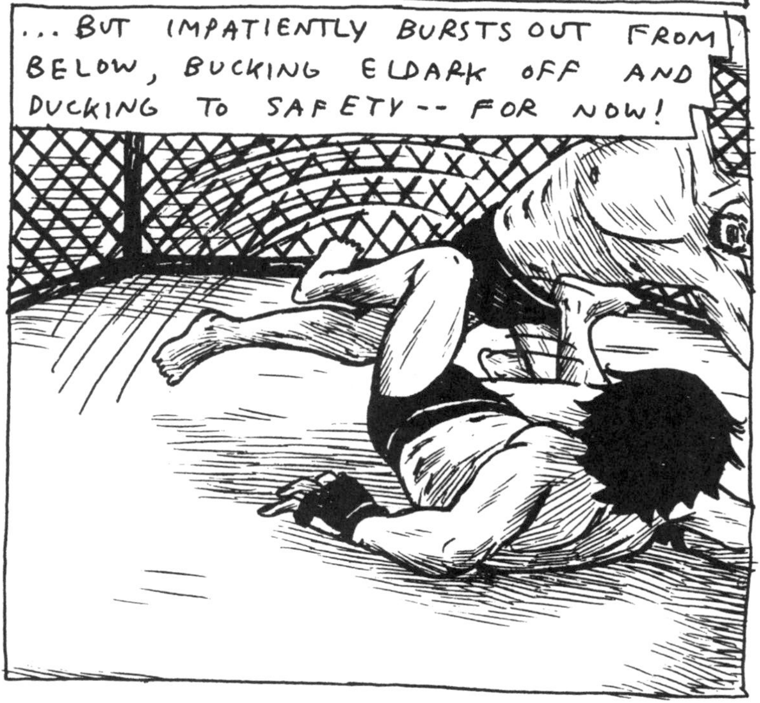
...BUT IMPATIENTLY BURSTS OUT FROM BELOW, BUCKING ELDARK OFF AND DUCKING TO SAFETY -- FOR NOW!

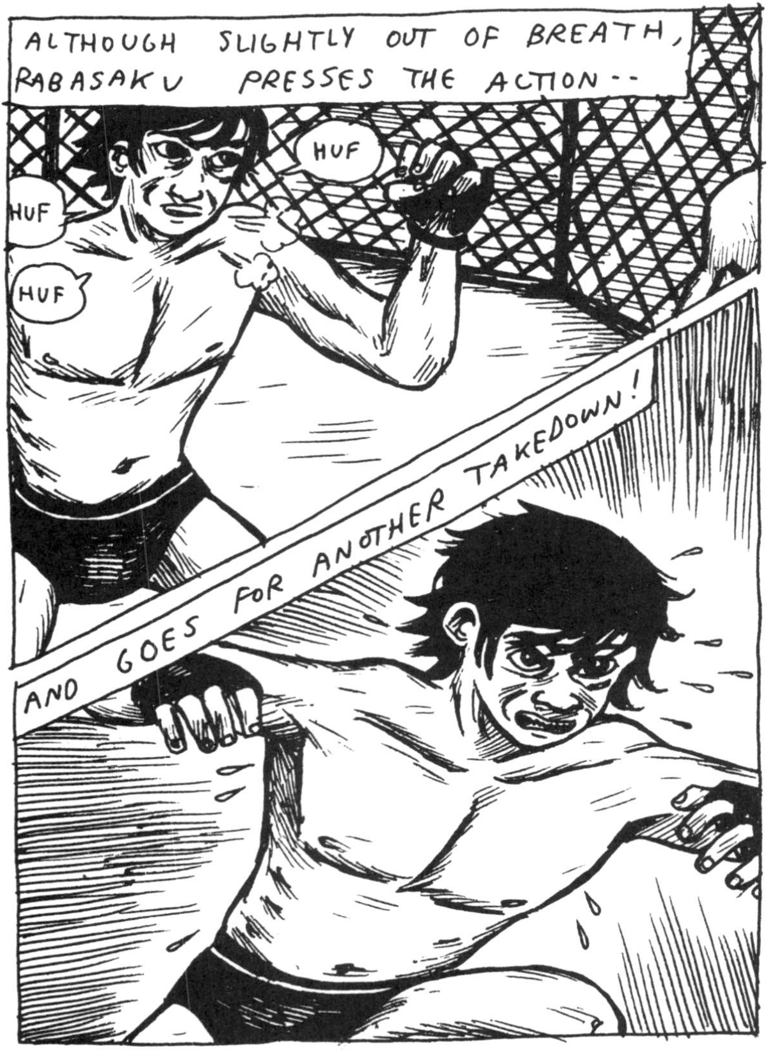
ALTHOUGH SLIGHTLY OUT OF BREATH, RABASAKU PRESSES THE ACTION--
HUF
HUF
HUF
AND GOES FOR ANOTHER TAKEDOWN!

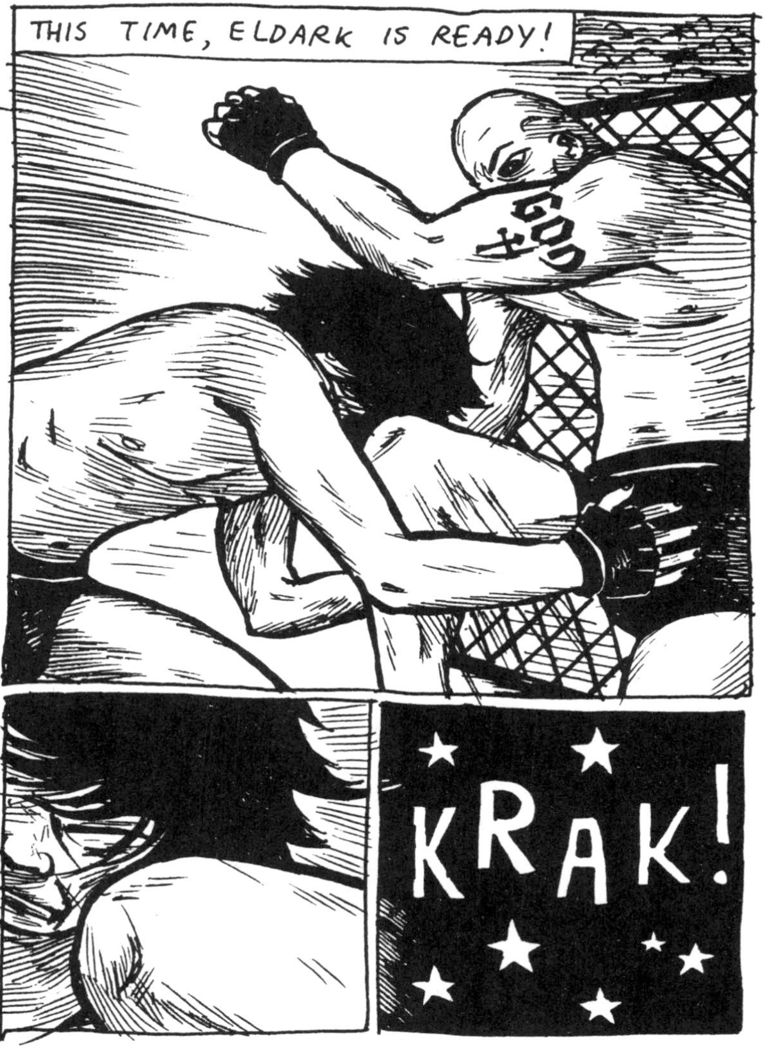
THIS TIME, ELDARK IS READY!
KRAK!

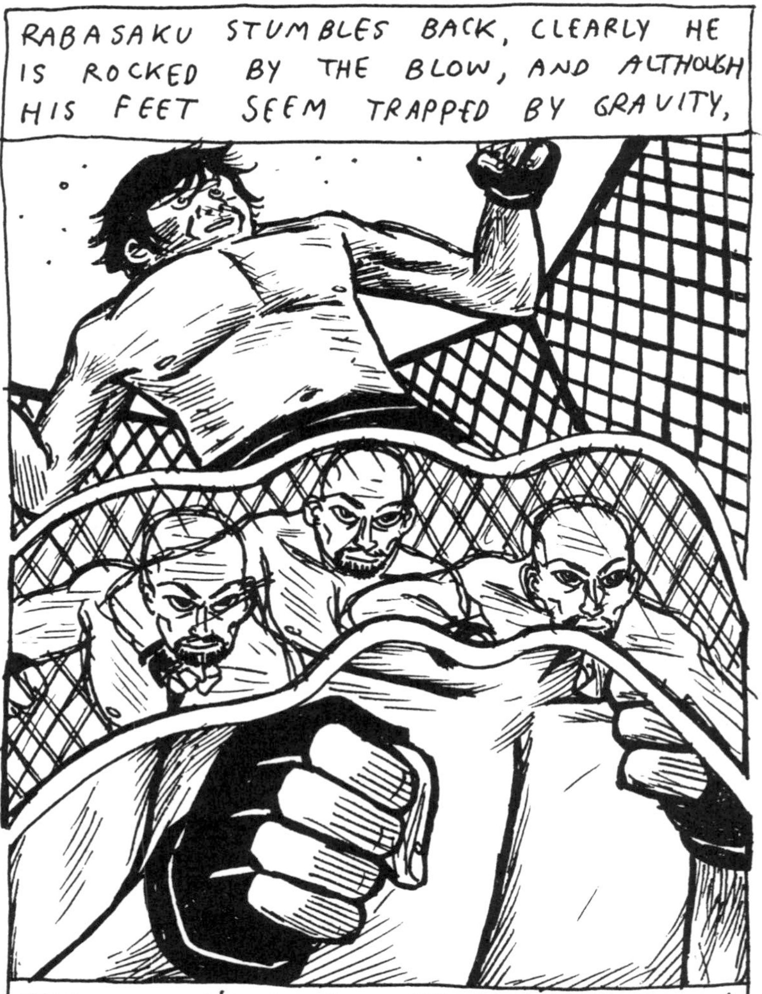
RABASAKU STUMBLES BACK, CLEARLY HE IS ROCKED BY THE BLOW, AND ALTHOUGH HIS FEET SEEM TRAPPED BY GRAVITY,
THE WARRIOR'S HEART IS STRONG, HIS FISTS UP!

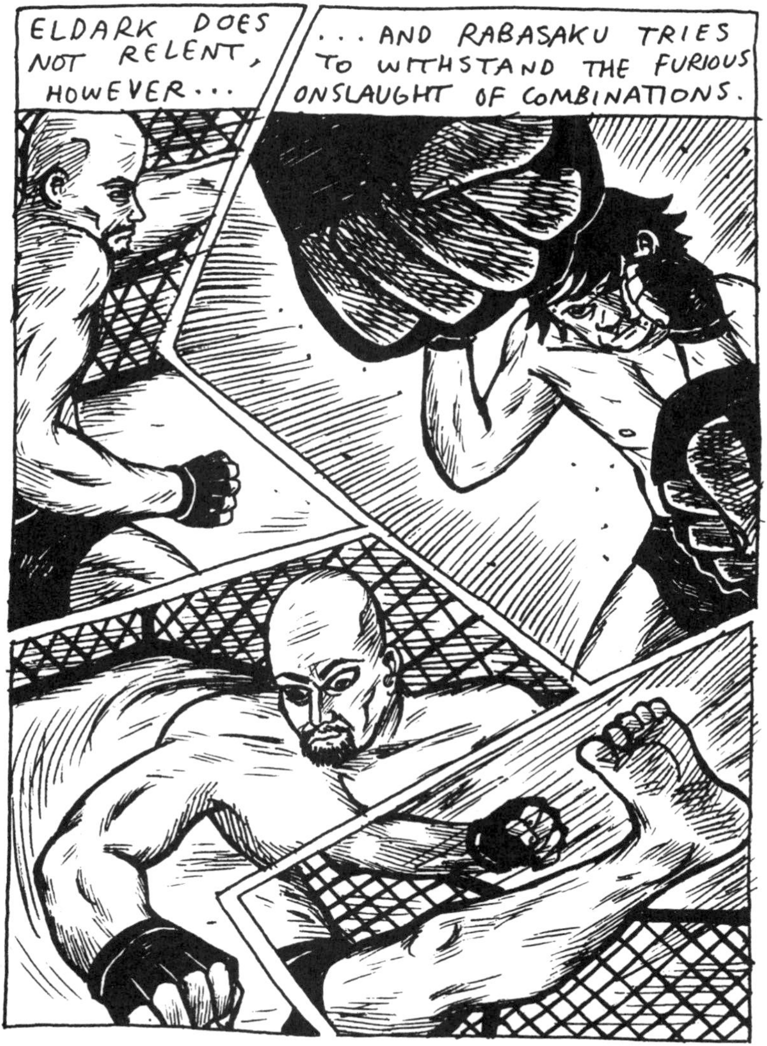
ELDARK DOES NOT RELENT, HOWEVER...
...AND RABASAKU TRIES TO WITHSTAND THE FURIOUS ONSLAUGHT OF COMBINATIONS.

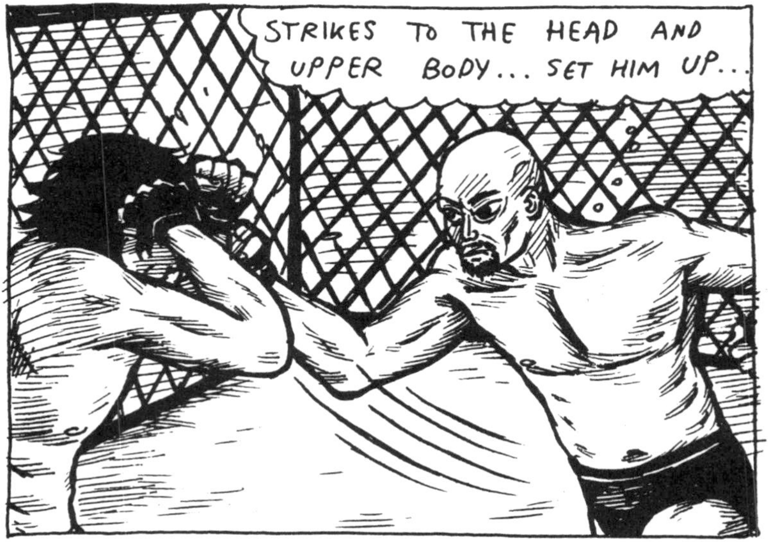
STRIKES TO THE HEAD AND UPPER BODY... SET HIM UP...

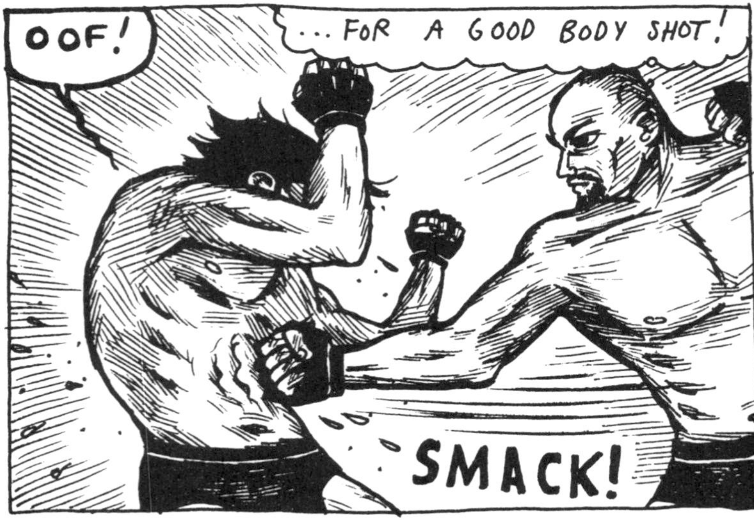
OOF!
...FOR A GOOD BODY SHOT!
SMACK!

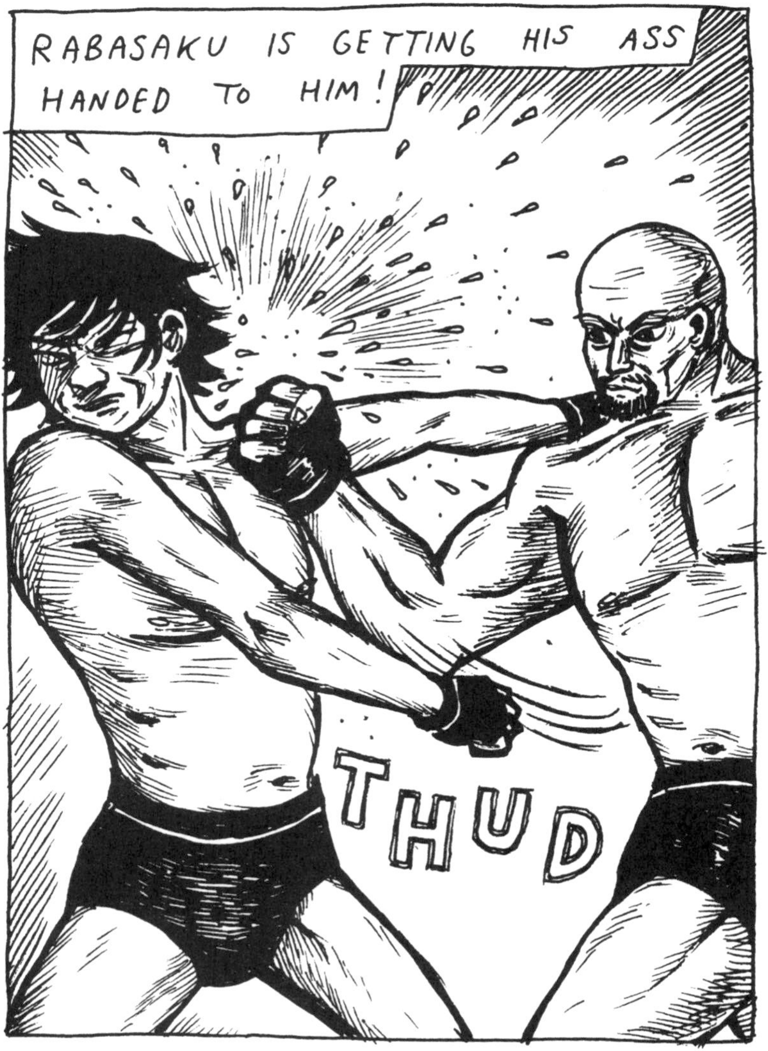
RABASAKU IS GETTING HIS ASS HANDED TO HIM!
THUD

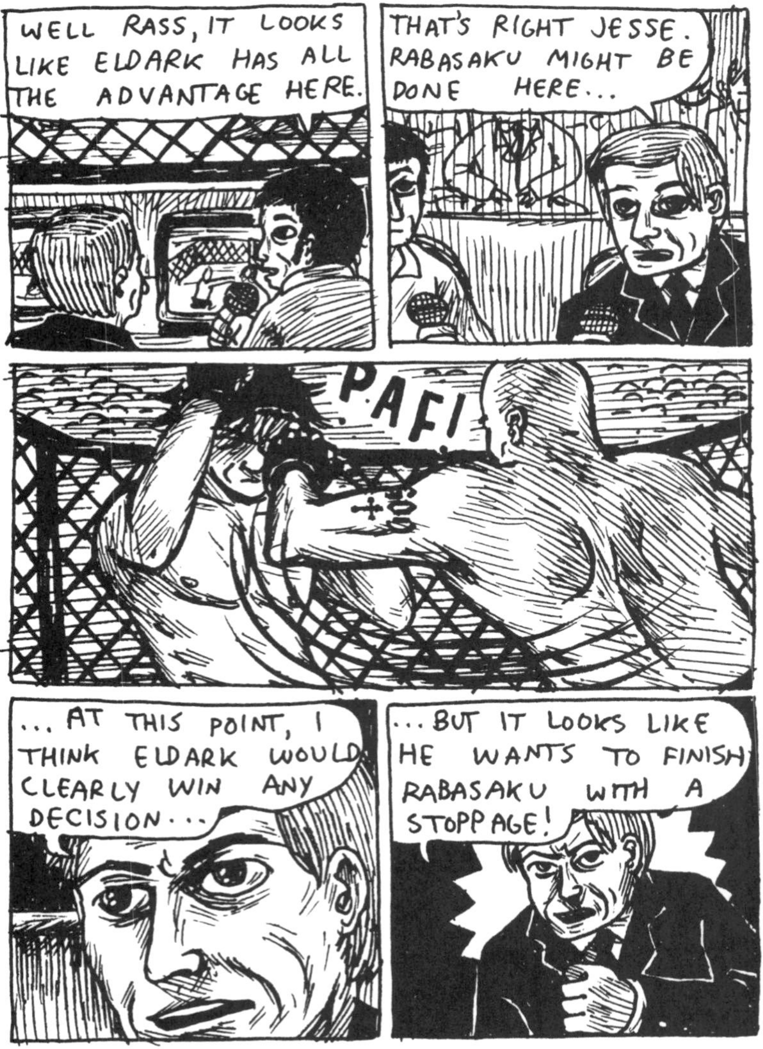
WELL RASS, IT LOOKS LIKE ELDARK HAS ALL THE ADVANTAGE HERE.
THAT'S RIGHT JESSE. RABASAKU MIGHT BE DONE HERE...
PAF!
...AT THIS POINT, I THINK ELDARK WOULD CLEARLY WIN ANY DECISION...
...BUT IT LOOKS LIKE HE WANTS TO FINISH RABASAKU WITH A STOPPAGE!

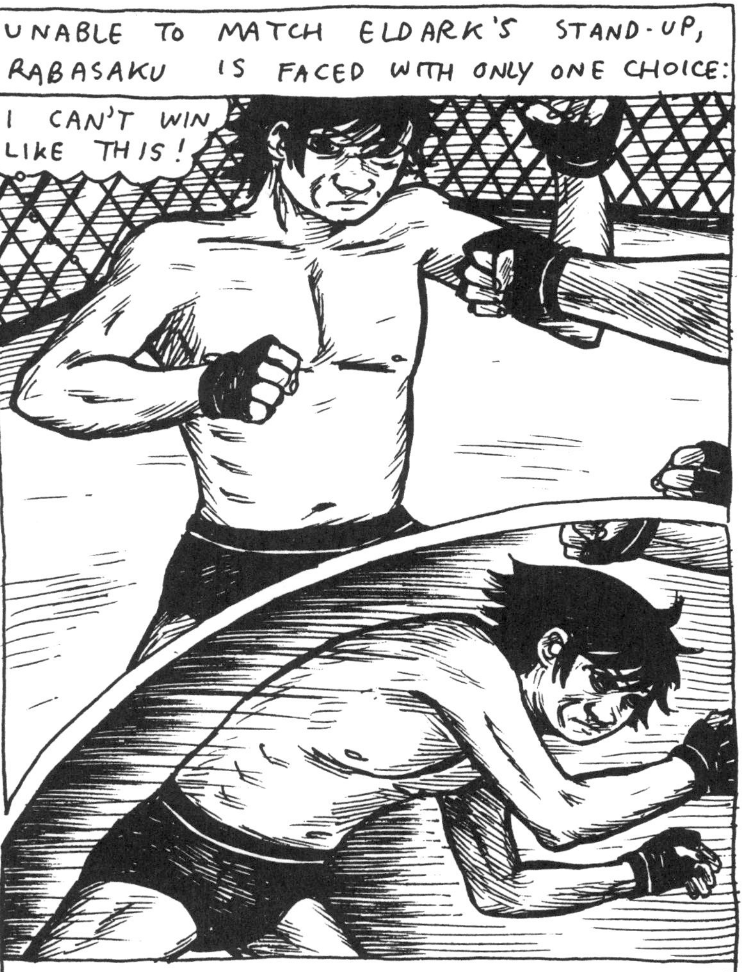
UNABLE TO MATCH ELDARK'S STAND-UP, RABASAKU IS FACED WITH ONLY ONE CHOICE:
I CAN'T WIN LIKE THIS!
I'VE GOT TO GET THIS FIGHT TO THE GROUND!

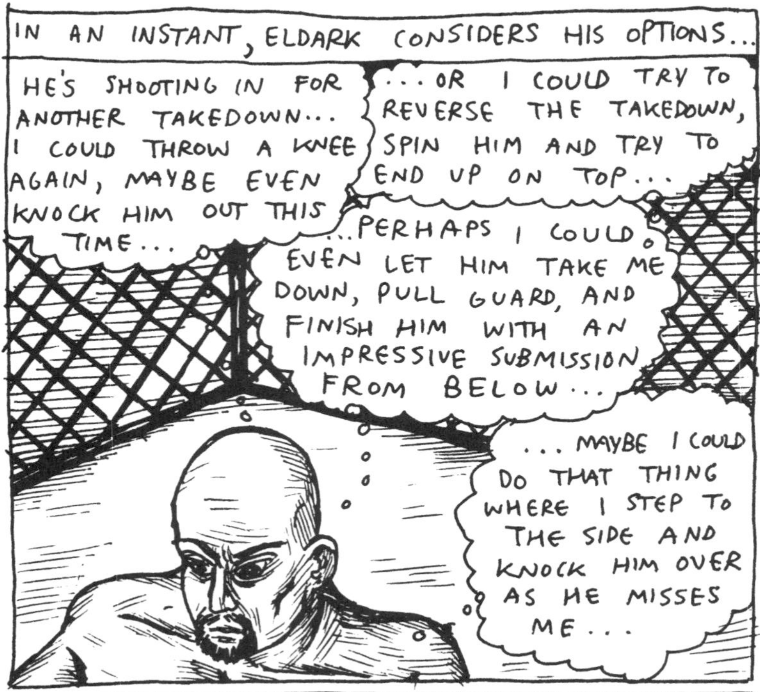
IN AN INSTANT, ELDARK CONSIDERS HIS OPTIONS...
HE'S SHOOTING IN FOR ANOTHER TAKEDOWN... I COULD THROW A KNEE AGAIN, MAYBE EVEN KNOCK HIM OUT THIS TIME...
...OR I COULD TRY TO REVERSE THE TAKEDOWN, SPIN HIM AND TRY TO END UP ON TOP...
...PERHAPS I COULD EVEN LET HIM TAKE ME DOWN, PULL GUARD, AND FINISH HIM WITH AN IMPRESSIVE SUBMISSION FROM BELOW...
...MAYBE I COULD DO THAT THING WHERE I STEP TO THE SIDE AND KNOCK HIM OVER AS HE MISSES ME...

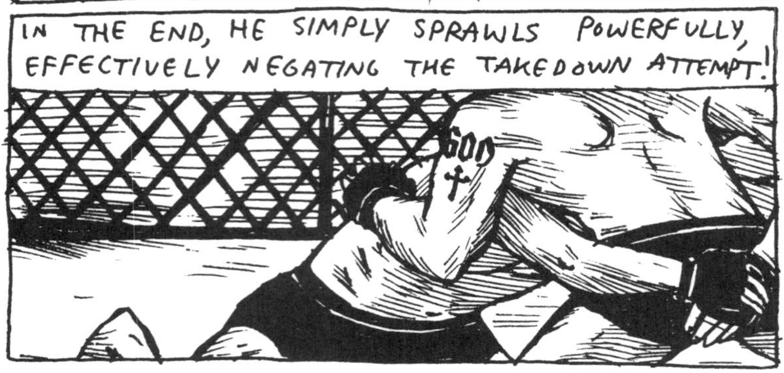
IN THE END, HE SIMPLY SPRAWLS POWERFULLY, EFFECTIVELY NEGATING THE TAKEDOWN ATTEMPT!
GOD

BREAKING OFF FROM HIS ATTEMPT, RABASAKU LOOKS FRUSTRATED.

THE TWO FIGHTERS TRADE PUNCHES...

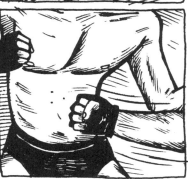

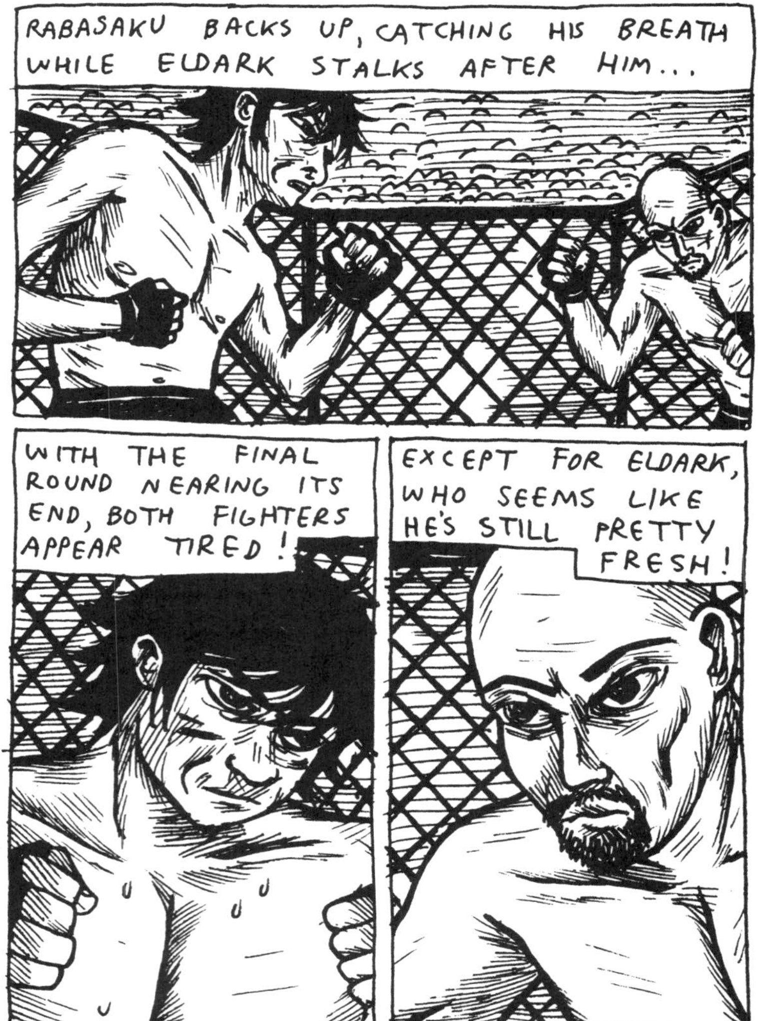
RABASAKU BACKS UP, CATCHING HIS BREATH WHILE ELDARK STALKS AFTER HIM...
WITH THE FINAL ROUND NEARING ITS END, BOTH FIGHTERS APPEAR TIRED!
EXCEPT FOR ELDARK, WHO SEEMS LIKE HE'S STILL PRETTY FRESH!

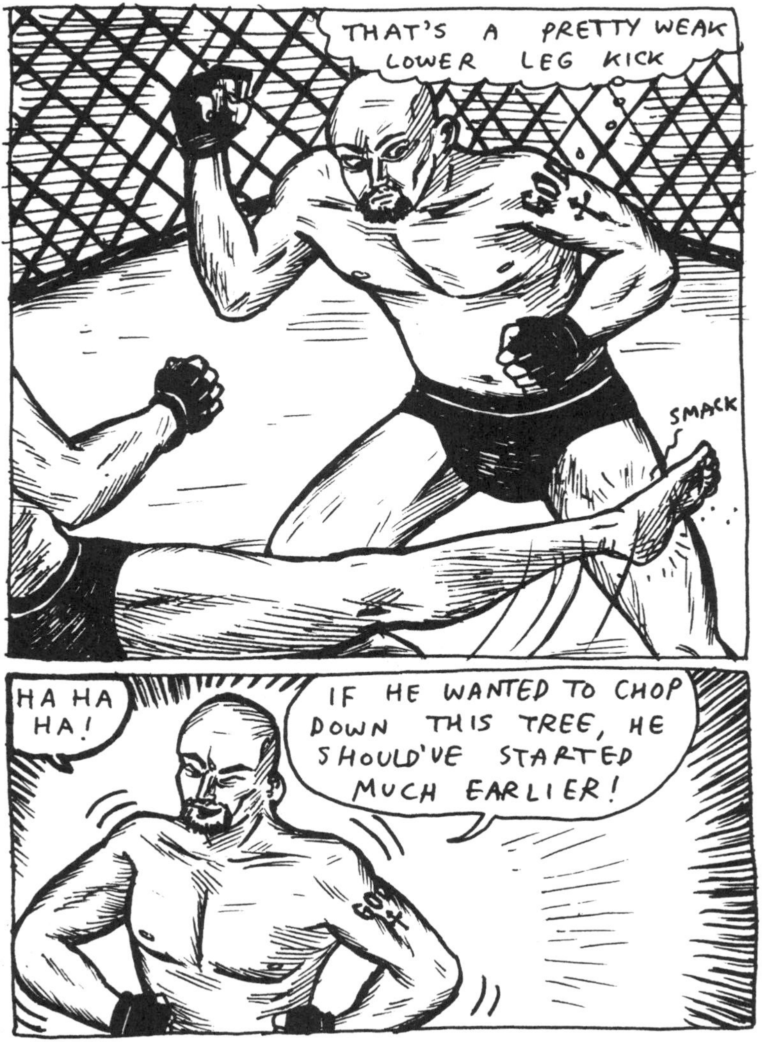
THAT'S A PRETTY WEAK LOWER LEG KICK
SMACK
HA HA HA!
IF HE WANTED TO CHOP DOWN THIS TREE, HE SHOULD'VE STARTED MUCH EARLIER!

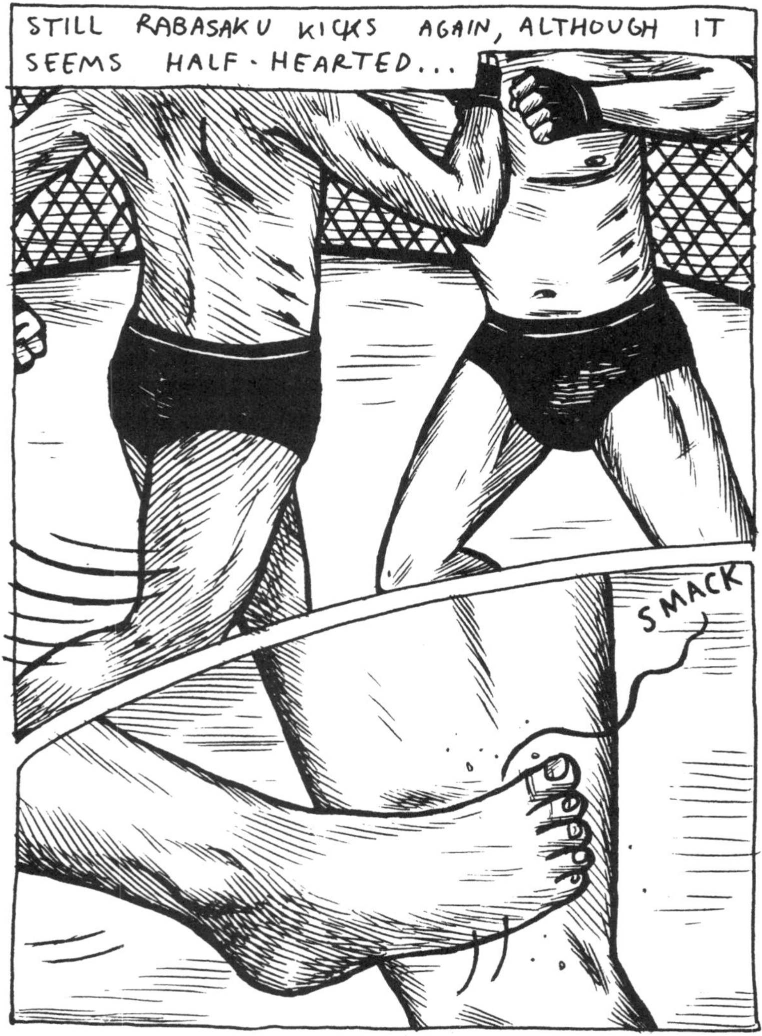
STILL RABASAKU KICKS AGAIN, ALTHOUGH IT SEEMS HALF-HEARTED...
SMACK

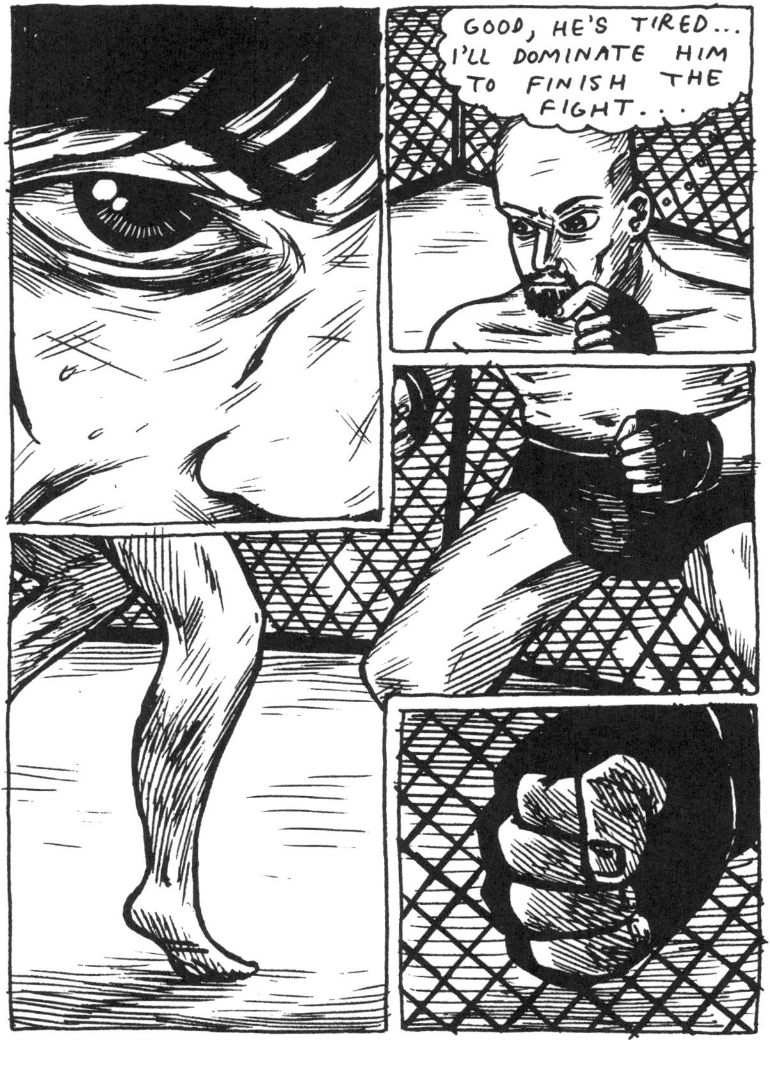
GOOD, HE'S TIRED... I'LL DOMINATE HIM TO FINISH THE FIGHT...

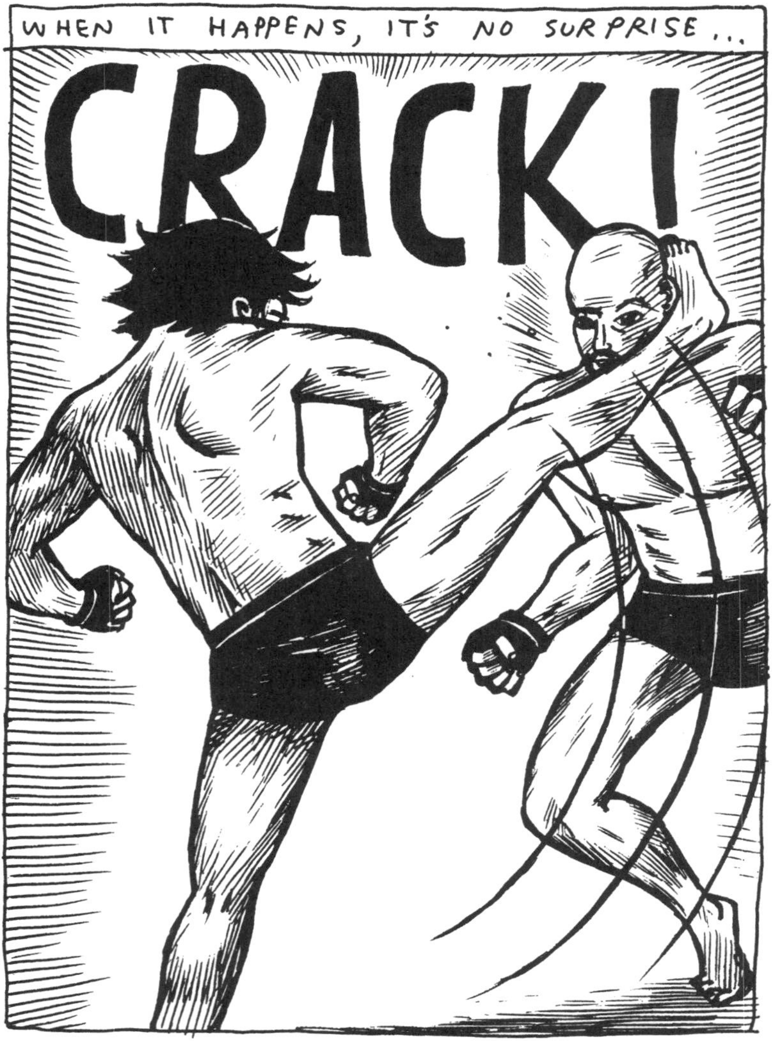
WHEN IT HAPPENS, IT'S NO SURPRISE...
CRACK!

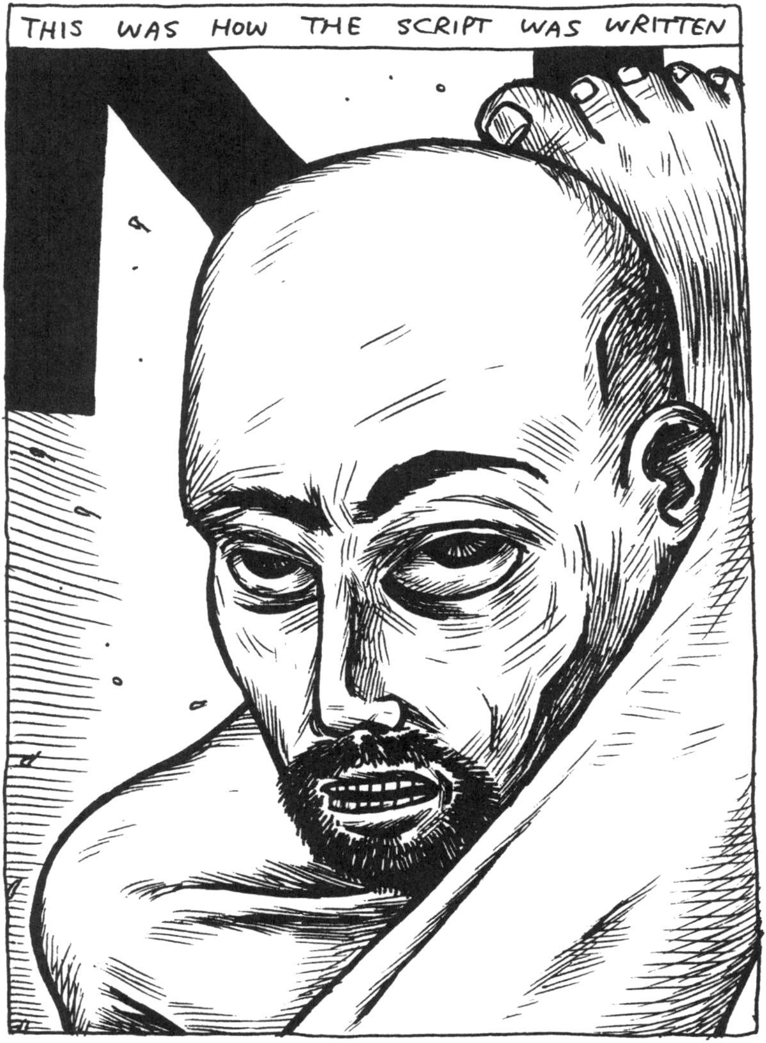
THIS WAS HOW THE SCRIPT WAS WRITTEN

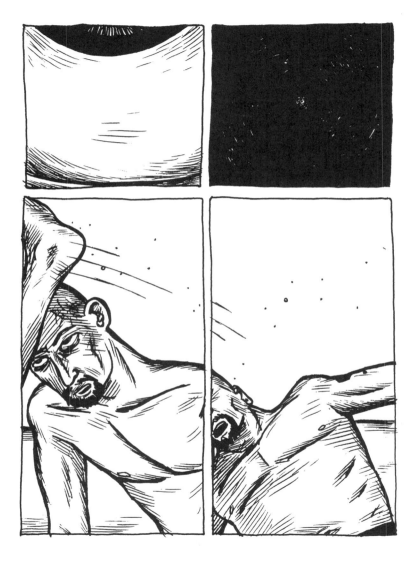

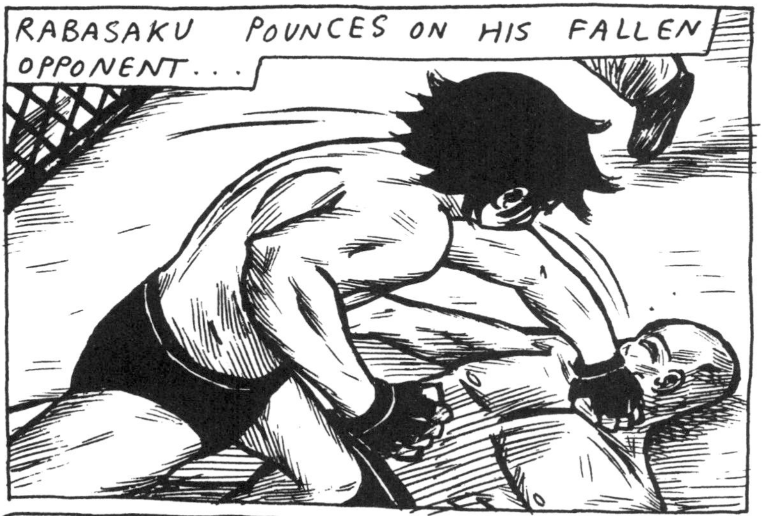
RABASAKU POUNCES ON HIS FALLEN OPPONENT...

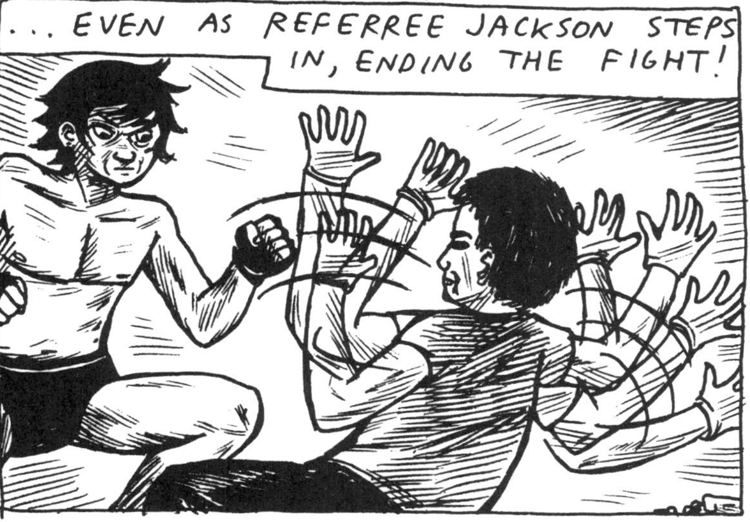
...EVEN AS REFERREE JACKSON STEPS IN, ENDING THE FIGHT!

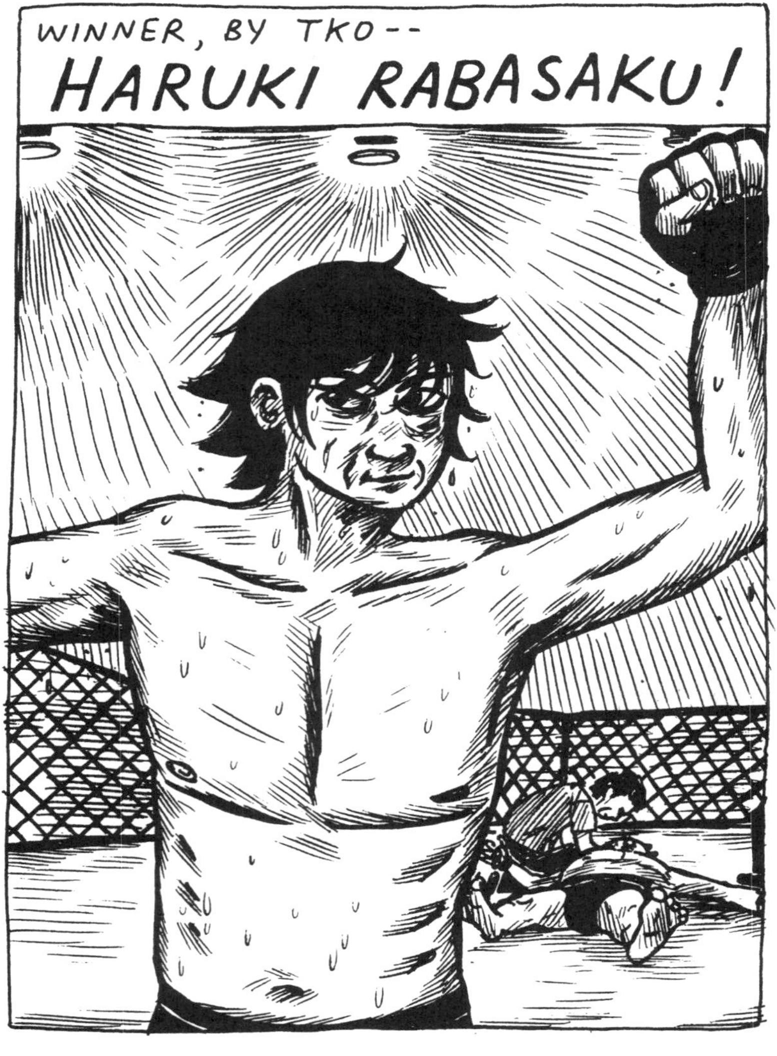
WINNER, BY TKO--
HARUKI RABASAKU!

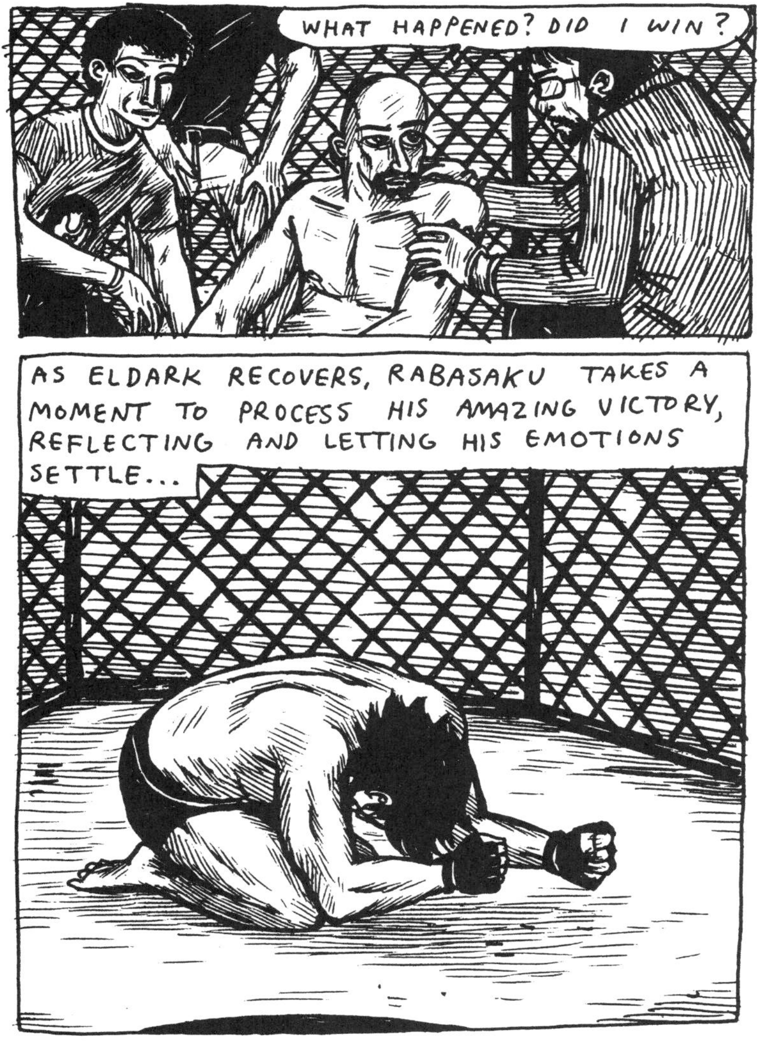
WHAT HAPPENED? DID I WIN?
AS ELDARK RECOVERS, RABASAKU TAKES A MOMENT TO PROCESS HIS AMAZING VICTORY, REFLECTING AND LETTING HIS EMOTIONS SETTLE...

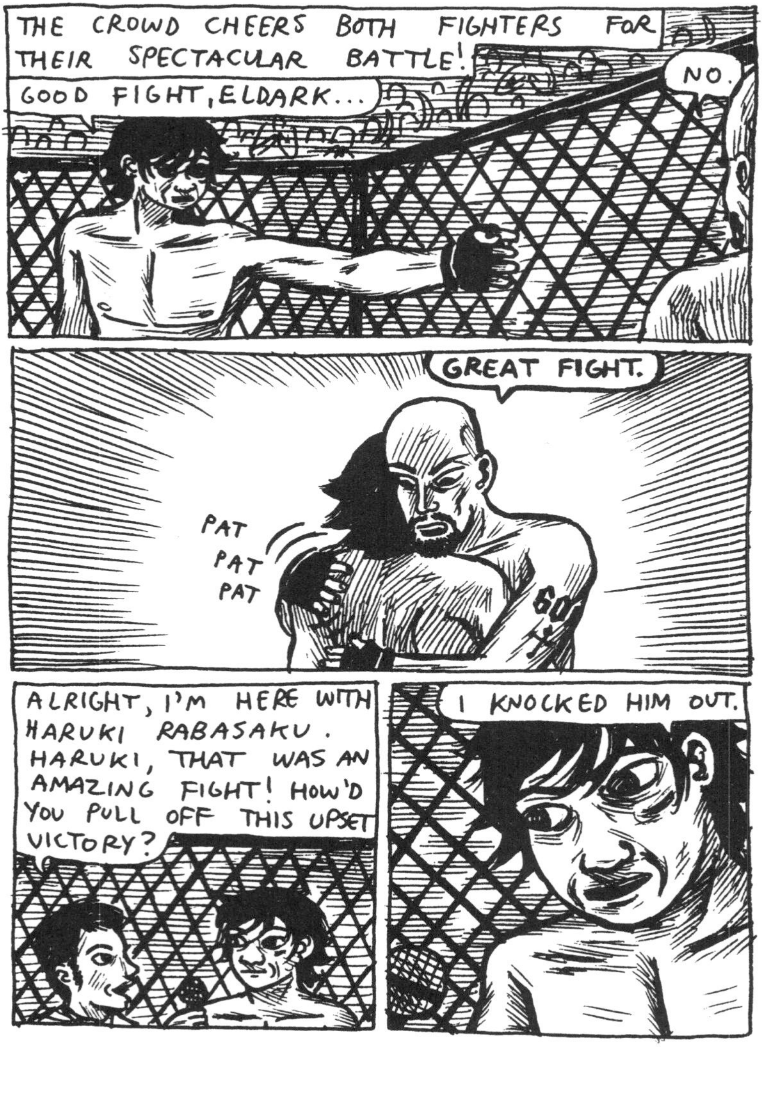
THE CROWD CHEERS BOTH FIGHTERS FOR THEIR SPECTACULAR BATTLE!
GOOD FIGHT, ELDARK...
NO.
GREAT FIGHT.
PAT PAT PAT
ALRIGHT, I'M HERE WITH HARUKI RABASAKU. HARUKI, THAT WAS AN AMAZING FIGHT! HOW'D YOU PULL OFF THIS UPSET VICTORY?
I KNOCKED HIM OUT.

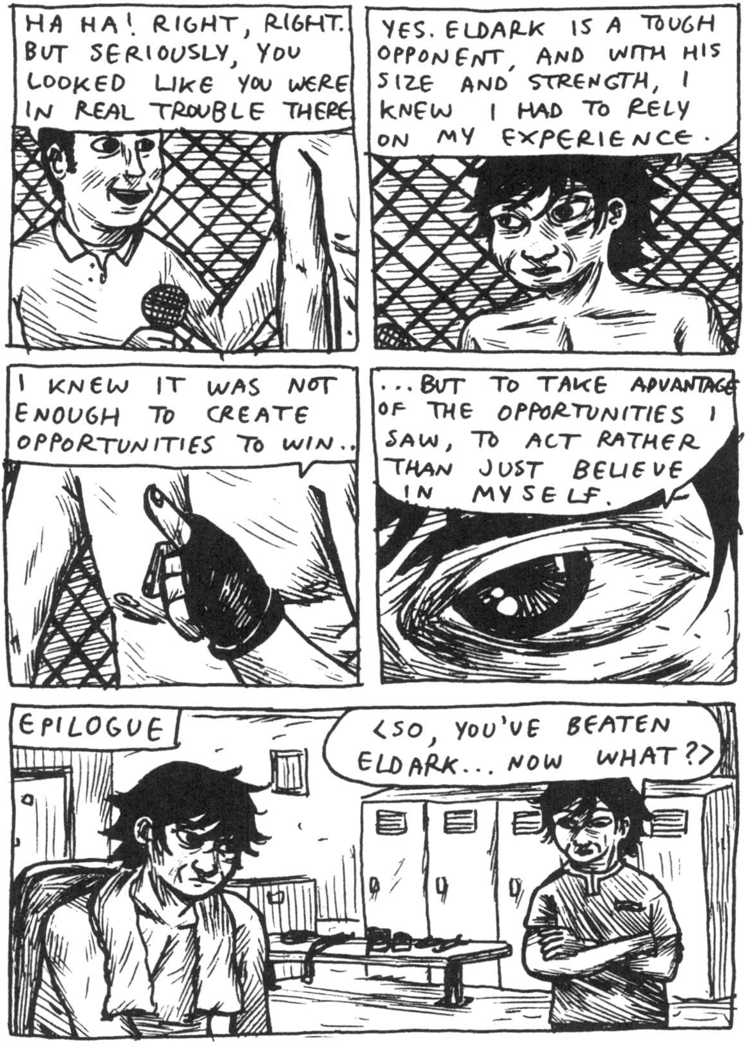
HA HA! RIGHT, RIGHT. BUT SERIOUSLY, YOU LOOKED LIKE YOU WERE IN REAL TROUBLE THERE
YES. ELDARK IS A TOUGH OPPONENT, AND WITH HIS SIZE AND STRENGTH, I KNEW I HAD TO RELY ON MY EXPERIENCE.
I KNEW IT WAS NOT ENOUGH TO CREATE OPPORTUNITIES TO WIN...
...BUT TO TAKE ADVANTAGE OF THE OPPORTUNITIES I SAW, TO ACT RATHER THAN JUST BELIEVE IN MYSELF.
EPILOGUE
<SO, YOU'VE BEATEN ELDARK... NOW WHAT?>

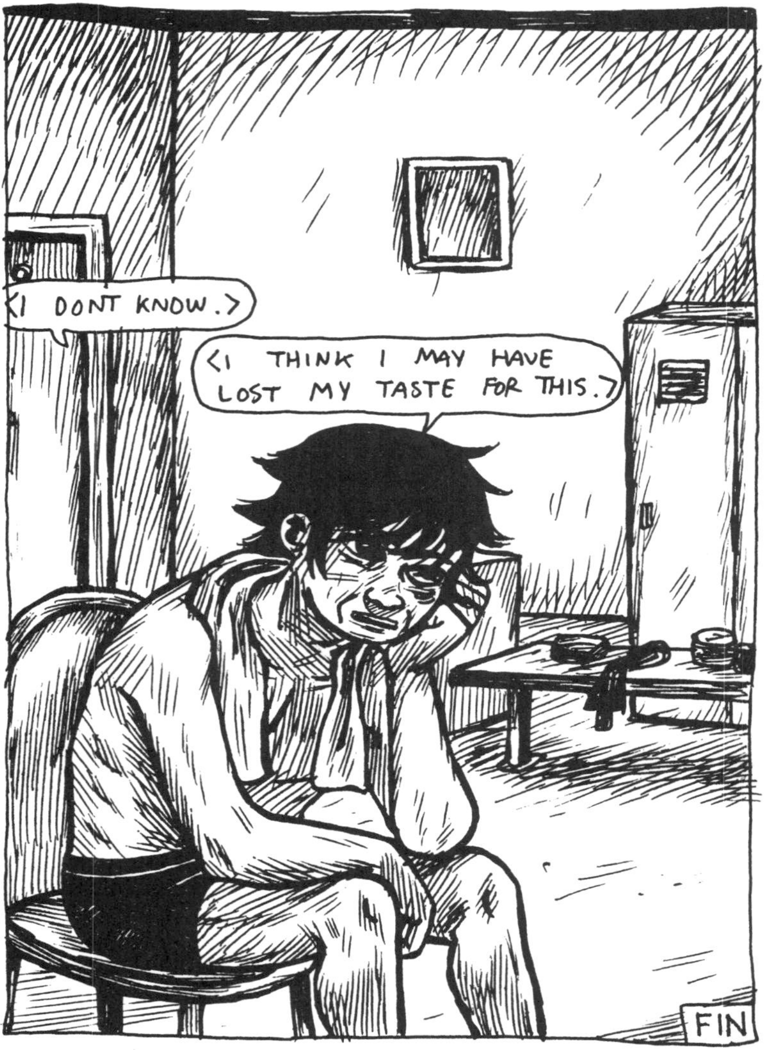
<I DONT KNOW.>
<I THINK I MAY HAVE LOST MY TASTE FOR THIS.>
FIN